PASTORAL PILGRIMAGE

Pastoral Pilgrimage

A sketch book of walks and churches on the Isle of Wight

by

Victor Vivian

First Published in Great Britain in 1994 by
Coach House Publications Ltd
Station Buildings
School Green Road
Freshwater, Isle of Wight
PO40 9BB

Sketches, maps and walk directions
© Victor Vivian

Historical notes on churches
© Robert Lumsden

© Coach House Publications Ltd

Printed by West Island Printers Ltd
Freshwater, Isle of Wight (0983 753161)

FOREWORD

When I was forty-six, I had a stroke, as a result of which, I lost the use of my right arm and the ability to walk normally; my speech was also affected. This meant that I had to abandon a small but flourishing picture-framing business and begin the long haul back to recovery.

After the first year I was able to walk almost normally, but my right arm was still affected. Following eighteen months of treatment, I spent some time at the Wolfson Rehabilitation Centre in Wimbledon where I made considerable progress; I cannot praise the staff too highly.

About this time I made two decisions. Firstly I would walk more than before and secondly I would learn to draw and paint with my left hand. (Using my right hand formerly, I had acquired some competence with water colours and had the satisfaction of selling some.) Naturally, my early efforts were discouraging - even unscrewing tubes of paint was far from easy. However, perseverence paid off and within two years of my stroke I could paint reasonably well with my left hand. Also, my walking gradually improved to the point where I was achieving up to eight miles a day. I began sketching scenes that appealed to me on my walks.

I then conceived the idea of drawing some of the many Island churches and devising a route, mainly of footpaths and lanes leading from one church to the next. Sometimes I was able to visit and pencil-sketch two or three churches a day which later formed the basis for pen and ink drawings. This book is the result.

As well as giving pleasure to fellow artists, hikers and lovers of old churches, I hope my efforts will give encouragement to others who might also be physically disabled.

Victor Vivian

ACKNOWLEDGEMENTS

I am greatly indebted to:

My family for all their help and especially to my brother Gordon for his companionship on some of the walks.

My chess partner Robert Lumsden who has spent much time and effort in compiling the historical notes which accompany each of the church drawings. In doing this he was greatly assisted by information contained in *Village Churches of the Isle of Wight* by Ron & Pat Winter, to whom acknowledgement is made.

Colin Kefford for help in publication.

Dr. Nigel Reid, Terence Sullivan, Colin Saunders and Gordon Collins for their encouragement, and all my many friends for their interest and support during the production of this book.

V.V.

All profits from the sale of this book will be given to the Wessex Heart Foundation.

CONTENTS

PILGRIM'S GUIDE

Before undertaking any of the walks your attention is drawn to the following points:

1. Paths across fields sometimes get ploughed up.

2. Signs sometimes get moved or changed. They can also become overgrown and difficult to locate.

3. Gates and stiles are sometimes removed.
Remember also that some stiles may be potentially dangerous to clamber over.

4. After heavy or prolonged rain, footpaths can remain very muddy for quite a long while. Be prepared.

5. Remember the Country Code. In particular -
    a) don't leave litter
    b) close all gates behind you
    c) don't drop lighted matches

6. The following walks are strenuous:
    Nos . 5, 7, 11, 19, 23, 29 & 31.
    (but I managed them! V.V.)

7. The walk from Shorwell to Chale does not pass any pubs or places of refreshment so you are recommended to take some 'rations' with you.

8. The walks consist of:
    Footpaths, farm tracks or Bridleways = 75%
    Major roads   = 3%
    Minor roads and lanes   = 22%

9. The entire pilgrimage covers a distance of 105 miles.

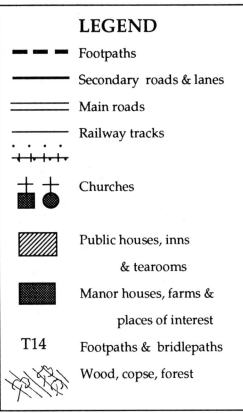

LEGEND

- - - Footpaths

——— Secondary roads & lanes

═══ Main roads

——— Railway tracks

Churches

Public houses, inns & tearooms

Manor houses, farms & places of interest

T14 Footpaths & bridlepaths

Wood, copse, forest

St Saviour's R.C. Church, Totland Bay

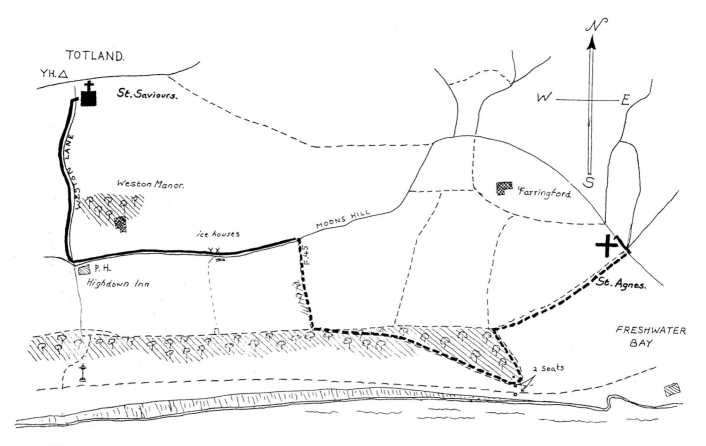

1. ST SAVIOUR'S, Totland, to ST AGNES, Freshwater Bay   2 miles

Leave St Saviour's and turn left up Weston Lane. Follow this lane to the Highdown Inn. Turn left past Weston Manor; notice the two Ice Houses on the left by the side of the road. Walk on, then take the footpath (F45) on the right-hand side. Continue uphill through trees to the top. (Warning: this path is usually muddy.) Bear left and in about 100 yards, turn right onto a narrow chalk path. In about 170 yards the path forks. Take the uphill path on the right to Tennyson Down. At the top there are many magnificent views. Walk on downhill on the short grass until you reach two seats (30 yards apart). Take the left path, keeping the fence to your right. About half-way down there is a walk-through stile. At the bottom you will find a gateway. Turn right through this and follow the path to the main road. St Agnes is nearby on your left.

Opposite St Agnes is Blackbridge Road. Follow this until it bends right. On the left you will find a sign: *Afton Manor Nature Reserve and footpath to Freshwater and Yarmouth.* Follow the path indicated, cross a wooden bridge and continue with the stream on your left to Afton Road. Turn left and after about 50 yards turn right down Footpath (F61) This shortly bears to the right and becomes part of the old Railway Track. Follow this for about 400 yards to the Causeway, with Tideways Cottage immediately opposite and Afton Thatch - a beautiful old cottage - within a stone's throw. Turn left, cross the River Yar bridge, pass Causeway Cottage and continue to All Saints.

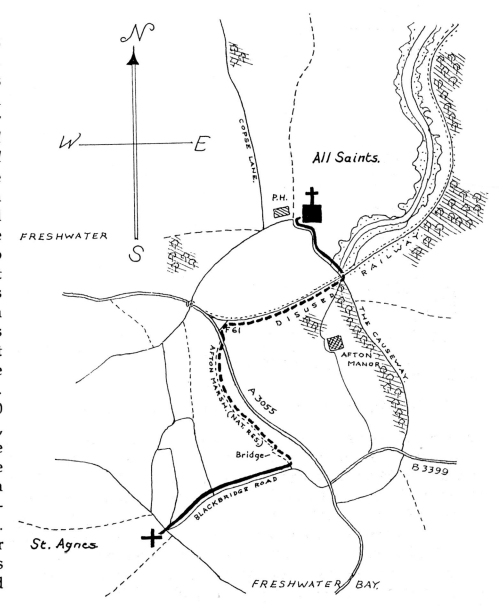

St Agnes, Freshwater Bay

St Agnes Church, Freshwater Bay, is unique in numerous ways:
(i) it is the only thatched roof church on the island, probably in England.
(ii) one reason for its erection was to provide a place of worship for holidaymakers.
(iii) its appearance springs from a draught water-colour executed by a local rector.
(iv) the ground on which it stands was given by the son of a Poet Laureate, i.e. Alfred Lord Tennyson.

Prior to its foundation in 1908, worshippers met in a corrugated iron structure in the Square nearby. This had proved to be cold in winter and virtually an oven in summer. So an appeal was launched to raise the necessary funds, and so great was the response that by August of the same year, the new church was consecrated by the Bishop of Winchester.

It was Lady Tennyson, the wife of the donor of the land, who suggested the church be dedicated to St Agnes, a young and beautiful saint whose story had always aroused her interest and admiration.

The church is a good example of re-cycling in the early years of this century, for the stone used in its structure came from a derelict farmhouse in the nearby Hooke Hill area. Proof of this lies in a stone inserted into the vestry wall which bears the date 1694. The reeds used for the thatching came from Norfolk and were supplied by a firm in Norwich. However, it was re-thatched in 1962 at a cost of £600. Seventeen years later, when it was thatched yet again, the cost was £9,000, which suggests that inflation is no new phenomenon.

The chancel screen is unique in that it is the work of a curate from the mother church of old Freshwater - the Rev. T G Devitt. The Porch was the gift of Lady Tennyson in memory of her mother.

The Ice Houses, Moons Hill, Totland

All Saints, Freshwater

All Saints, Freshwater, is almost certainly one of the oldest churches on the Island, which means that it was active for four hundred years before it was given to the Abbey of Lyre in Normandy after the Norman Conquest.

There is a high probability that the central nave of today was originally the simple Anglo-Saxon church. Justification for this belief is that on three of the nave piers, one can see the typical long and short quoins used by pre-Norman builders. The missing fourth quoin would have been removed during extensive alterations in the 19th century. The 13th and 15th centuries had also seen large-scale development, and it was in the second of these periods that a tower was incorporated into the west wall; its closed pointed arch and recessed window are unique amongst Island churches. Notice that the 12th century font (restored last century by a member of the Worsley family) stands at the west end in its own railed off baptistry. The fine window in the west wall is another memorial to a Worsley, namely Charles Fortescue of the Colonial Service.

The very earliest memorial tablet here is also near the west end, and it is dedicated to Ann Toppe, daughter of Thomas Arkell, a member of the Privy Chamber of Queen Elizabeth. She narrowly escaped a gruesome death during the Irish rebellion of September 11.

Rectors are listed without interruption back to 1286. One was arrested in 1394 for smuggling wool. Another after only two years became Archbishop of York in 1531. Thomas Wolsey, the famous Cardinal, was Vicar of Lymington and a friend of his. Be sure to observe a small brass - that of Adam de Compton - who was one of the Island's Militia Commanders in the 14th century.

This church is rich in Victorian stained glass. Particularly beautiful is the three-light window behind the altar. Alfred Lord Tennyson, the Poet Laureate, and his wife used to worship here regularly. Such was his fame that he was interred in Westminster Abbey, but his wife's remains lie in the churchyard.

Afton Thatch, The Causeway, Freshwater

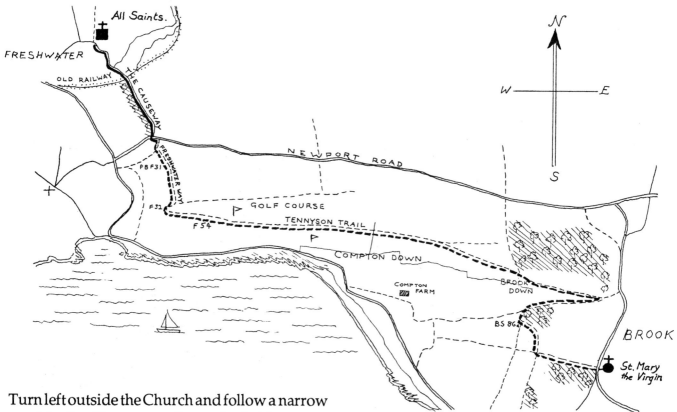

Turn left outside the Church and follow a narrow road to the Causeway. Cross the bridge, pass Afton Thatch and continue with woods on your right and open fields on your left, until you reach the main road at Afton Barns (a recent development). Turn left along the main road for about 30 yards and then bear right down Manor Road. Continue for about 80 yards, then left along PB F31 until you reach the Golf Course. Go through the stile at the end and continue up a steep chalk hill (F32) on the right and at Bridle Way F54, turn left for a steady uphill climb for about 1.25 miles At the end of the golf course you

will find a gate. Go through this and after another 1.25 miles, after descending the chalk track, turn sharp right and continue uphill until you reach a water trough. Take the left fork just past this and continue downhill through a gateway. After about 100 yards turn left down BP (BS86a), down a winding lane. When the BP ends, take the lane on your left. Ahead of you is Brook House, once the home of J. B. Priestley. (You will see the Church spire nestling in the trees.) Continue in the lane until you reach the Church.

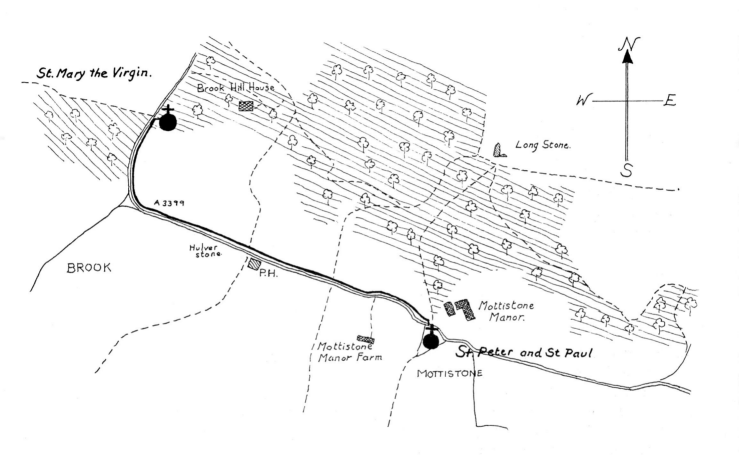

Come out on to the road and turn left. After about 200 yards take the Brighstone Road (A3399) passing through Hulverstone. Keep to the road which will lead to Mottistone after about a mile.

St Mary's, Brook

V. Vivian

One wonders why St Mary's was erected so far from the village of Brook which it serves. Have the villagers, over the course of time, moved nearer to the sea, or could a suitable site capable of bearing so much weight not be found near the village?

No one can say, but we do know that a fire in December 1862 destroyed all the earlier structure except for the tower. The fire had been caused by a faulty stove igniting the wood of a newly-built gallery, the planks of which came from the barque *'Cedrene'* which had been wrecked off Brighstone.

The architect of the new church tried to imitate the Gothic style of the 13th century, though the original building undoubtedly went back further. This had for many years been a dependent chapel of Freshwater Church, and it was only after much wrangling that it obtained independent status in the 18th century.

Fortunately certain things survived the fire in addition to the steeple. The registers, for example, go back to 1653, and the list of incumbents goes back to 1297, though there are a few gaps in the record.

The stone head of a lion, much the worse for wear, is on a window sill. The piscina in the sanctuary was also saved; likewise the window in the east wall depicting the Crucifixion. Following World War I it was adapted as a war memorial.

At the west end of the church are painted boards

Freshwater Bay

recording the valiant exploits of the men of the Brook Lifeboat who saved 263 lives from 1860 to 1936. Be sure to find the touching message of appreciation and gratitude from the Captain of a Spanish ship, the crew of which was rescued on November 18th 1904.

The pulpit is made basically of Caen stone, and the trefoil font of Sicilian marble.

Brook Hill House

St Peter & St Paul, Mottistone

St Peter & St Paul Mottistone was built in the 12th century for the use of the inhabitants of the Manor House. There were very considerable renovations in the 15th and 19th centuries; nevertheless it has preserved its medieval character despite the well meaning intentions of Victorian architects and builders in 1863.

There is little coloured glass here except for a two-light window depicting the two saints of the dedication. This means that the greenery of the churchyard may be glimpsed through the remaining clear glass windows, which make the church unusually light.

A manorial chapel was built in the 15th century by Robert Cheke. This family owned the manor house nearby from the middle of the 14th century until 1623. One of them, Sir John Cheke, became tutor to Edward VI and later Secretary of State. Another did not do so well; in fact he thoroughly mismanaged the estate and had to sell it.

The new owner was Robert Dillington of Knighton Gorges. This man was a "social climber" and purchased a baronetcy. His grandson, the second baronet, inherited the Manor House, and it is the wife of this man who has a Table Tomb in this church and another at Newchurch. Which, one wonders, contains the worthy lady's remains?

An interesting feature of this church is its lighting by candles in brass candelabras; also the cedar planks in the chancel roof. These came from the 'Cedrene' which was wrecked locally on her maiden voyage from Bermuda. There was no loss of life as all the passengers, including 200 convicts who were being returned after helping to build a dockyard, were able to wade ashore.

Look for the beautifully carved Jacobean pulpit, also a long inscription in Latin round an oak screen in the Cheke chapel. It proclaims the virtues of General "Jack" Seeley who, as a young man, was a member and Coxswain of the Brook Lifeboat, but who later became a Cabinet Minister and the first Baron of Mottistone. His ashes lie before the chapel altar. Another stone in the sanctuary commemorates "Jack's" son John, who was a brilliant architect and was eventually appointed Surveyor of St Paul's. He left the estate to the nation under the care of the National Trust.

Interior of Mottistone Church

Immediately opposite the church porch is the footpath to Longstone and the downs. Keep to this path, uphill, for about 300 yards, then take the right fork and continue up and round to steps, and to a wide track. Cross this and take the narrow track opposite. Continue uphill until you reach the Longstone, where there is a seat. Skirt left, keeping the downs on your right and follow a chalky path. After about 150 yards, turn right up a grassy path and in another 50 yards, right again along a narrow track. Look out for a right-hand turn up a very narrow path (which bears left). Take this and make a steep ascent to a stile. Cross this and turn right, making your way up to the top of the hill and part of the Tennyson Trail, then downhill to the road. Turn left down Lynch Lane. After about .75 mile, turn left up Public Bridleway (CB16B). After about 600 yards there is a house. Pass this and take the next footpath on your right. Look carefully, as this is easily missed. Look for a yellow arrow on the stile. Leaving the woodland, take a footpath through the middle of a field. Cross several stiles and after a wooden bridge bear right. This path leads to Winkle Street. At the end turn left to find the church on the right in about 50 yards.

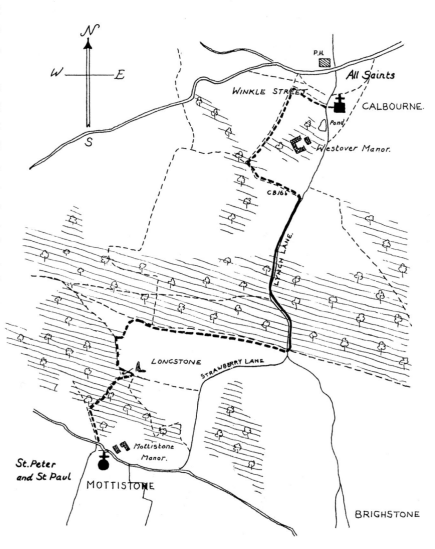

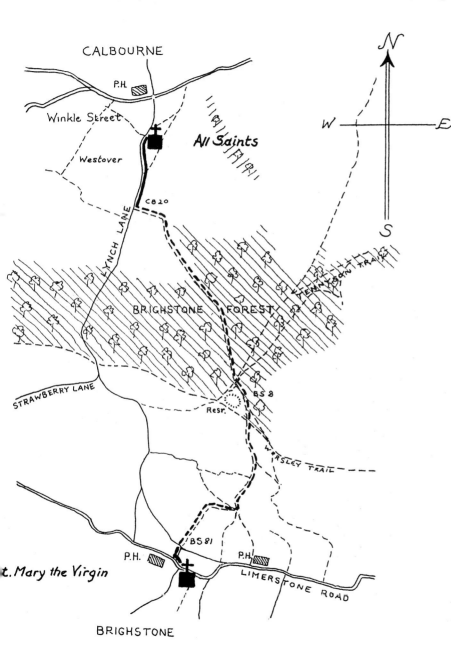

On leaving the Church, turn left and proceed up Lynch Lane past Winkle Street and Westover Manor for 800 yards to footpath CB20 on your left. Take this path uphill for about 200 yards, then right through a gate. Continue uphill, through a field, until you reach a gate to the forest. Go through this and continue straight on up. After about 1000 yards you will find BS8. Carry straight on until it forks to the right and you will come to the Worsley Trail. Cross over, continue on a narrow track down a steep hill and through an old gate until you come to a stile on your right. This is marked with arrows. Follow the blue one (do not cross the stile). After about 15 yards bear right and continue until path forks (approx. 10 yards) Take right fork and continue along and downhill. You will have views of Brighstone ahead of you and a fine view of Tennyson cliffs in the distance. The track now becomes a Bridleway which goes downhill through trees, eventually reaching a road. Opposite you will find North Street with its old thatched Post Office. Turn left into the main road and the Three Bishops public house is just ahead and the Church about a hundred yards away.

All Saints, Calbourne

Although there is little evidence today of the original structure, All Saints, Calbourne was established at a very early date as there exists a record of a grant of land being made by King Egbert in 826; also the church is one of five mentioned in the Doomsday Book.

The present building is basically 13th century, though many alterations and rebuildings took place between the 15th and 19th centuries. Much of the church was badly damaged by fire in 1683 and was not rebuilt until 1752.

This checkered history has led to the church developing into an unusual shape. You will also notice that the long chancel rises up to the altar by a series of steps. Behind the altar is an elaborately carved reredos based upon Leonardo da Vinci's Last Supper. Blue curtains either side of the altar hide coloured tiles. The ceiling is also tiled and the remainder of the east wall is painted blue. One wonders whether this preponderance of blue was meant to direct the thoughts of worshippers heavenwards.

The north transept and the burial vault beneath it were rebuilt in the 19th century by the Simeons of Swainston. This would account for the ten mortuary tablets of the Simeon family ranged in the transept.

Despite Swainston having been owned by royalty and nobility, there is no indication here of the fact. This absence encourages intriguing speculation. The south transept is also bare,

although it once contained a tomb which never held mortal remains. A clue is to be found in a brass on the wall dated 1379. It testifies to the existence of a young Montacule who was accidentally killed by his father, William Earl of Salisbury, while they were jousting together.

We know that the south transept was rebuilt and enlarged in the 18th century and it was then that the tomb was probably destroyed. It was one of thirteen which the grief-stricken father had had placed in village churches in his domains.

The arches of the North Porch, both inner and outer, are pseudo-Norman, having been built in the Victorian era. The first rector, one Malger, was the uncle of William the Conqueror and the Archbishop of Rouen. Another rector of the 16th century, one Christopher Hampton, became Archbishop of Armagh in 1613.

Longstone

St Mary the Virgin, Brighstone

Many would agree that St Mary's Brighstone is one of the most beautiful of the Island's village churches. Although alterations have been made since it was built in 1190, they in no way detract from its charm.

Inside, look for the Norman arches of the north side of the nave, and you will notice that pillars supporting the arches have tilted slightly. This is thought to have been caused by the great weight of the original stone slated roof. Beneath one of the arches, you will find the 14th century octagonal font. It is carved on all sides and is large enough for a child to be completely immersed, which was earlier deemed to be necessary.

South of the nave are the remains of the Limerstone Chapel. This was built by the Tichbornes of Limerstone in the 15th century. They lived less than two miles to the east; originally they had their own Oratory (c. 1250), served by a warden and three chaplains of the Augustinian Order. It seems to have been suppressed during the late 14th century. All that remains of the Limerstone Chapel are remnants of a spiral stairway which led to a screen behind the altar; also a piscina in the south wall of the chancel. This was a stone bowl with a drain for disposing of water used to rinse the chalice. The chapel's altar stone is also in the chancel.

It is remarkable that three former rectors have become bishops. Look out for the neatly inscribed wall plaque giving details about them. One was

Westover Manor

Thomas Ken who has given us several well known hymns. He lived in the 17th century. Then there was Samuel Wilberforce, the son of the celebrated champion of the slaves. He became Bishop, first of Oxford, then of Winchester. Lastly there was George Moberly who became Bishop of Salisbury and who, before his Rectorship (1867-69) was Headmaster of Winchester School for 31 years. The local inn was renamed after them in 1973 - Three Bishops.

Looking down into Brighstone

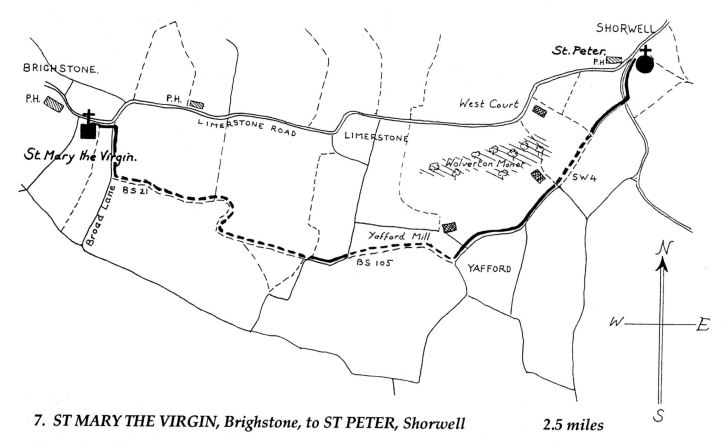

7. ST MARY THE VIRGIN, Brighstone, to ST PETER, Shorwell   2.5 miles

On leaving the Church turn left through the churchyard on to the main road. Take the next turning on the right (Broad Lane) to Waytes Court (150 yards), where you take footpath BS21 on the left through a gate. Continue straight on (over 3 stiles) 700 yards, when the path turns to the right.

Keeping the hedge to your left, continue over one more stile and 600 yards further on you come out onto a lane. Continue along this lane for about 200 yards (past the Island Fish Farm)

when you will find a footpath BS105 on your right. Follow this path to Yafford Mill. At the Mill turn right uphill for 100 yards, then turn left. Continue along lane until you pass Wolverton Manor on your left. Take Public Bridleway SW4 (from where you can see the church spire). In about 400 yards you come out to a narrow lane. Continue for about another 300 yards then turn left on to the main road, and the church is at the end.

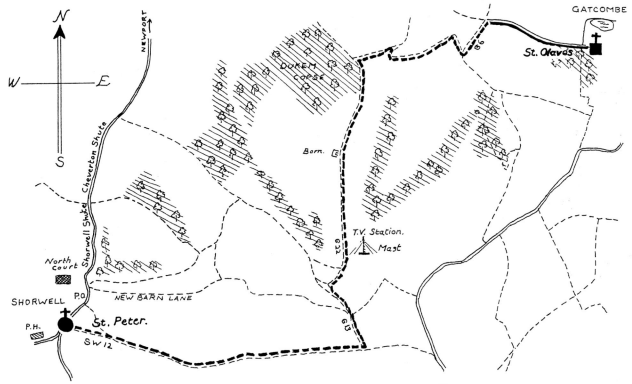

8. ST PETER, Shorwell, to ST OLAVE, Gatcombe — 3.5 miles

With the church on you right hand side, take the first turning on the right (SW12) which leads uphill; continue until you come to a gate. Go through this and turn to the right. Continue for about a mile and then turn left up Public Bridleway G13. Pass through a gate and continue up a steep ascent to your right towards the mast. (On a clear day both Culver cliff and Tennyson cliffs can be seen.)

Arriving at the top, continue along, keeping the mast to your right. Over a fence, turn to the right, then over a three-bar stile next to a gate. Opposite is Public Bridleway G22. Take this past the mast (which is about 1,000 ft high and has 15 supporting wires housed in massive concrete slabs). After about a mile, enter a copse and take the path on your right (G22) Gatcombe. Continue for about 300 yards and make for the signpost downhill to your right. Continue downhill on chalky path to a gate (G7). Go through this and a further 200 yards downhill brings you to a right-hand turn, past farm buildings (on your left). Turn right at the track's end and after a further 50 yards left down Bridleway G6. About 500 yards along, this Bridleway ends with a right turn onto a lane. Follow this lane for about 700 yards and you will see the church at the corner.

St Peter, Shorwell

Uniquely, St Peter, Shorwell is rectangular and symmetrical, although the north aisle was built about 1100 as a private chapel for the residents of the manor of North Court. The nave and south aisle were added in later years. Two doors, exactly opposite to one another at the west end, reinforce the effect of symmetry, likewise the steeple being centrally placed.

Inside, notice that the floor slopes gently upwards, and in addition there are two breaks of two steps stretching right across the building. This raises the altar about five feet above the lowest part at the steeple end. The 15th century pulpit and the lectern are placed in the centre, with the pews sited around them.

Though there are three manor houses in the vicinity, North Court has been most concerned with the development of the church.

Understandably most of the memorials are to members of families who have occupied the manor house. Look particularly for the tomb of Sir John Leigh who was deputy Governor of the Island, and that of his wife, Elizabeth, a Dingley from the neighbouring manor of Wolverton.

An unusual feature is the wooden, portable altar used by General Sir Willoughby Gordon when he was on active service in the Peninsular War of 1809. Over it is a copy of a painting of the Last Supper, the original of which has now been returned to Iceland. The wooden framework of the altar encloses exquisitely carved figures of two of the Gospel writers.

Another thing to look for is the unusual Roof Beam. Normally this contains a representation of the Crucifixion, but this portrays the risen and glorified Lord with St Michael and St Gabriel on either side. Two stone corbels representing Sin and Death support the beam.

Note also the 15th century mural which depicts scenes from the life of St Christopher as well as his martyrdom. This is probably contemporaneous with the Godshill Lily Cross.

There is an unusual brass in the east wall of the north chancel. It commemorates the two wives of Barnabas Leigh; one of them had fifteen children, and the other was barren but possessed "rich, rare, virtues".

Yafford Water-Mill

St Olave, Gatcombe

St Olave's, Gatcombe goes back to the 13th century, but it is highly likely that even in Saxon times there was a private manorial chapel here. Today, little remains of the 13th century building, but the simple stone font has survived.

The building had been constructed by the descendants of William Fitstur, and they were later known as the de Esturs. In the 17th century it was purchased by one of the Worsleys of Appuldurcombe, and a number of their descendants became Rectors here. In the chancel you will find a memorial tablet to one of them - James and wife and seven children.

What little stained glass there is is worth inspection. One window depicts several angels and dates back to the 15th century, making it the oldest on the Island. In contrast, the east window in the chancel is by the Victorian William Morris and his associates.

On the north side of the chancel is the effigy of a crusader, carved in oak, with a heavenly messenger by his ear, and his feet resting on a dog. It probably represents a member of the de Estur family who went on one of the Crusades. Incidentally, there are a number of strange and romantic tales surrounding this memorial. Even the dog is said to come alive every hundred years and dance in the moonlight on the pathway to the church.

The Tower, re-built comparatively recently, very obviously dominates the church; indeed, some might feel that its bulk is a trifle out of proportion. The south porch, built in 1910, contains timbers from a ship of the line which participated in the Battle of Trafalgar.

Over the entrance to the porch is a grotesque face, undoubtedly of great age - the object of it being to keep out evil - hardly a Christian concept.

In the churchyard, there are headstones bearing many well known names. One is that of Brannon, the family who excelled in making prints, and these are much valued today. The two narrow archways in the east wall of the nave either side of the chancel arch were made in 1917 at the instigation of Sir Charles Seeley who created the County Library Service. There is also a splendid memorial and effigy to his eldest son, Charles, who was killed on active service in Palestine in 1917.

New Barn Cottage

Outside the gateway to the church is the beginning of a climb through trees, Public Footpath G11 on your left. Take this and continue round a double bend. Continue straight on down Bridle Road G8 which is Brook Lane and which has a small ford at the end. Crossing the ford, turn right into a main road and continue for about 0.5 mile. Then turn left up Public Bridleway G15A which is Hollow Lane. Continue uphill for nearly 0.5 mile, then turn right along G5A. Continue down through a farm, then turn right along a road for about 200 yards. Turn left into Public Bridleway G15, through two more gates and then turn left on to the road and continue for about a third of a mile. Turn right by Ivy Cottages down Footpath SW42 to Kingston. Follow this path and turn left on to the road where you will find the church 100 yards along on your right.

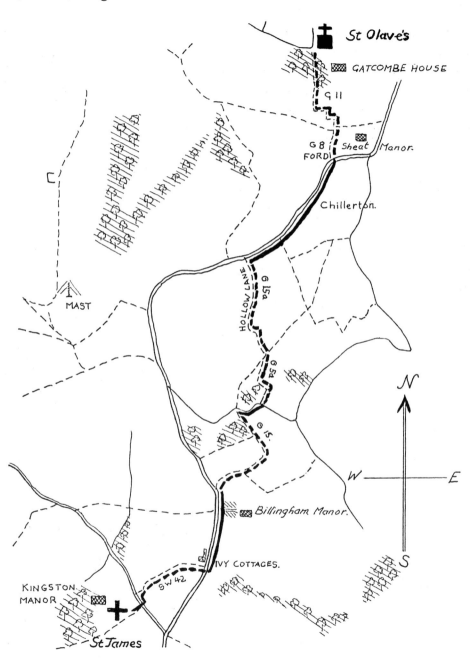

Continue along the road for about 400 yards. Turn right at Emmett Hill and continue for about 0.5 mile to where the main road forks round to your left. Continue straight on up Chale Lane. Just before Newman Lane look for a large herd of deer on your right. At the next right hand bend is Westside Lane (on your left). Take this and about 100 yards on turn left, over a gate on to a footpath. Continue to the end of this, then turn right on to a main road. You will find the church after about 0.5 mile.

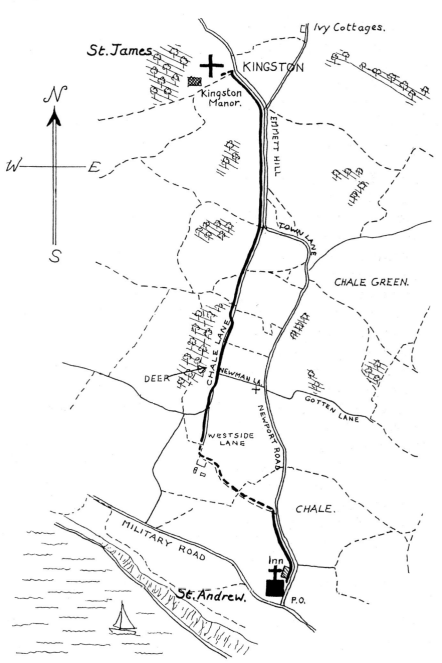

St James, Kingston

We hear much today of redundancy; well, here at St James, Kingston we have a redundant church.

For centuries a medieval village church on this site had served as a private chapel for the Lords of Kingston Manor whose residence was close by. It was also used by their tenants who were mostly agricultural labourers.

The church spire, Shorwell

In 1872 it was extensively re-built, although it retained its medieval charm. Since then, however, with fewer people being employed on the land, its congregation dwindled to such an extent that it was eventually declared surplus to the spiritual needs of the area. In consequence, services were discontinued, furnishings of worth were removed, and a padlocked iron covering was placed over the porch door. Presumably from time to time vandals gained entry and wrought havoc, as the interior today is a scene of chaos.

Fortunately, as is obvious, the exterior is in a state of good repair. Drainpipes and guttering seem to have been renewed, parts of the walls have been re-pointed, and broken tiles replaced. The graveyard, too, appears to be cut regularly.

Looking down to Kingston

St Andrew, Chale

St Andrew, Chale is the most exposed of the ancient churches on the south coast of the Island.

There is an unusual, almost sinister absence of trees in the churchyard; instead there are innumerable graves of those who have perished on this dangerous strip of coast - the inscriptions on many long since indecipherable. One example of maritime tragedy is that of the 'Clarendon', a fully rigged ship which sank with heavy loss of life in 1836.

Erected in the early 12th century, the church consisted originally of a nave and chancel only; then later the same century, the south manorial chapel was added by the Lord of the Manor. This was soon to be lengthened; then, three centuries later, there were more extensions and the tower was added. Finally, in the l9th century, along with many other ancient churches, it underwent extensive renovations.

Though some deplore the zeal of the Victorian builders, it must be said that without their industry, many churches on the Island and elsewhere would either be in ruins or be too dangerous to use.

Judging from the monuments extolling their virtues, this church has been blessed with many pious and hard working rectors. A lamp in the sanctuary of the manorial chapel keeps alive the memory of one such, the Rev. Charles William Heald (died 1930) who was Rector from 1885 to 1926. There is also a tablet to his wife who seems to have served the parish with unstinted devotion.

There is a large tablet also in the sanctuary of the manorial chapel to the son of a Rector, i.e. Major General Sir Henry Worsley of the Bengal Army who died in 1841 aged 73. From the inscription, it seems tht he was a magnanimous humanitarian as well as a distinguished military man.

A wealthy American, George Arnold Hearn, a descendant of former Rectors, has donated five beautiful windows, the clock and two bells in the steeple, and the organ. The last is dedicated to his daughter and the windows to his father who died in America. Because of the explanatory nature of the inscription, the tablet is, inadvertently(?) a memorial to himself.

Lower House, Chale

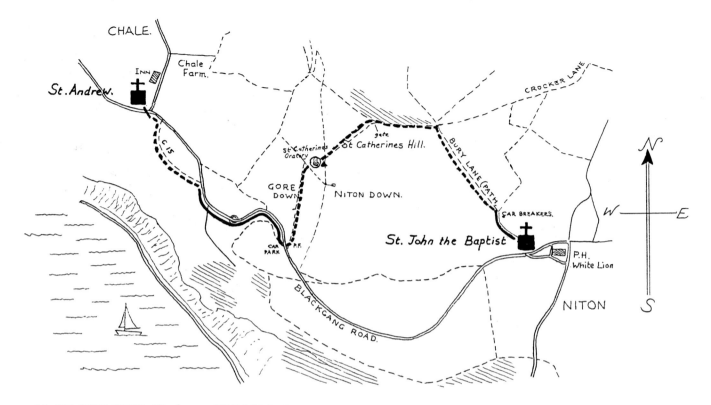

11. ST ANDREW, Chale, to ST JOHN THE BAPTIST, Niton 2.5 miles

On leaving the church, continue up main road for 50 yards and you will see a sign (Pedestrians to Blackgang) on your right. Take this path (uphill for 50 yards), then along a footpath C15 on your left. Follow through to main road and turn right. Follow the main road, round roundabout uphill and a wide right hand bend. Just past this bend to the right is a scenic car park and on the other side of the road is a footpath to St. Catherine's Oratory. Take this footpath up a steep gradient to the Oratory. After looking at this, cross over two stiles next to a triangulation pillar and continue to your left. Partially skirt the field and

then take the next stile on your left, halfway along the field. Having crossed this there is another stile a little way further to your right in another fence. Go over this and go down over hill to a gate in the bottom right hand corner of another field. Go through this gate and on to a footpath. Continue on this for about 300 yards, then take a grassy path on your right. (It becomes steep and stoney downhill.) At the bottom (about 700 yards) you come out to a narrow lane (with a car breakers' yard to your left.) Pan Lane and Niton Church is at the end on your right.

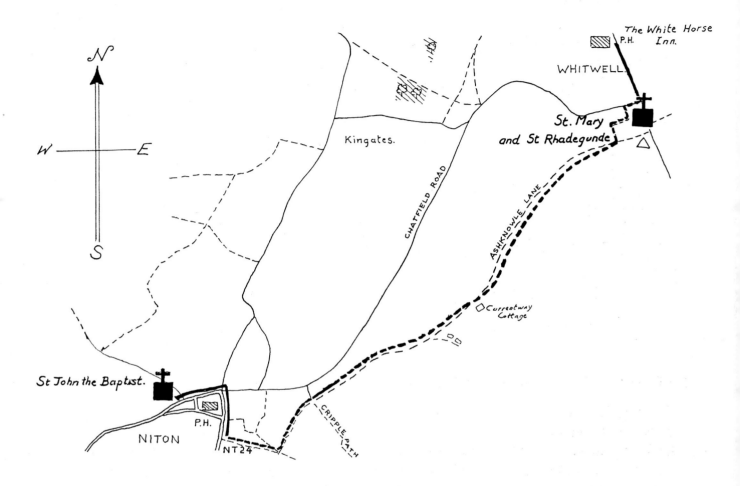

12. ST JOHN THE BAPTIST, Niton, to ST MARY & ST RHADEGUNDE, Whitwelll   *1.5 miles*

Leaving the Church, turn left and in 100 yards or so you are at cross-roads. Turn right here and take the second footpath (NT24) which is on your left. Go straight on at the sign-post and you come to a road. Turn right here. The road becomes a track. Continue on this, climbing and descending for about a mile. This is Ashknowle Lane. Just before its end, take a very narrow footpath on your left, through trees. After a bend to the right you come to the rear of Whitwell Church.

(You might like to eat at the White Horse Inn about 100 yards down the High Street.)

St John the Baptist, Niton

St John the Baptist, Niton is probably the darkest church on the Island. Its gloom is due partly to the smallness of its windows, partly to the number of yews and other trees in the church yard.

The church was already well established at the time of the Conquest, and shortly afterwards, along with five others, it was given over to the Norman Abbey of Lyre. When founded in Saxon times, it was dedicated to St Michael. Why he was replaced by John the Baptist is unknown.

The present churchyard was originally the village green, the base of the ancient market cross may still be seen. The nave is the oldest part and is mentioned in the Doomsday Survey of 1086, but this and other parts were restored as late as 1864.

The north aisle is 12th century and the south is 14th century along with a new chancel and the south porch. The tower was added two centuries later, as was also the gun chamber, for at that time each parish church had to house a cannon in case of an invasion by the French.

Inside the church, on the south wall, is a memorial tablet to George Arnold who died in 1806. There is some justification for believing that he was related to Dr Thomas Arnold, the celebrated headmaster of Rugby School, and father of the poet Matthew Arnold. George Arnold's wife, Henrietta, is commemorated by a double window in the Lady Chapel. These two lights depict Jesus with a group of children and Jesus raising a child

from the dead. Henrietta lived to the age of 92, dying in 1849.

Another double light shows six episodes in the life of John the Baptist. It perpetuates the memory of the Kirkpatrick family of Scotland, though how this occurs so far south is not clear. Possibly a branch of the family sought a more amenable climate on the Island.

A brass plate at the west end records the gift of a pair of bells in 1931 by Elizabeth Leith, in memory of her mother, Mary Charlotte Julia Leith, and Elizabeth's brother, Robert. Mary came from Northcourt (Shorwell) and was a friend of the poet Algernon Swinburne (see Bonchurch: St Boniface).

The Oratory

St Mary and St Rhadegunde, Whitwell

V. Vivian

It is hard to believe that this church, dedicated to St Mary and St Rhadegunde at Whitwell, was originally two separate memorial chapels. One was built in the 12th century by the de Estur family, for use by their tenants in the manor of Wydcombe. This was dedicated to St Rhadegunde. The other was erected in the 13th century by the Lord of the Manor of Stenbury for his tenants along part of the Undercliffe. This was dedicated to the Blessed Virgin Mary.

Before we go any further, it may be of interest to say something of the rarely mentioned St Rhadegunde. She was born in Germany in the 6th century, but was taken a captive by the French. Amazingly she eventually became Queen, but lived a most saintly life and founded an Abbey in Poitiers. She was renowned for her compassion and gentleness, particularly towards captives, no doubt because of her own early experiences.

The two chapels remained functioning separately until the 16th century, when the dividing wall(s) was removed. Obviously this necessitated some changes and restoration at the time, but much more was done in 1868 by the Victorians whose zeal in such projects seems to have been unlimited.

Inside there is a very fine carved oak screen between nave and chancel. Unusually both chancels are carpeted and this fact, coupled with impressive brass chandeliers, gives an atmosphere of warmth and intimacy. Two members of

the Oliver family are remembered here by beautiful stained glass windows. The first is in St Rhadegunde's chapel, and is in memory of Sir Robert Oliver, a high ranking officer of H.M. Indian Navy, who died from sunstroke in Bombay in 1848. The second, in the north wall of the nave, commemorates a former vicar - the Rev. Robert Oliver, who died in 1912. Both windows have depictions of Christ as a central theme.

The pulpit (17th century) is probably the work of a village craftsman of great skill, and near this is a modern brass of intricate design in memory of an officer of the Royal Warwickshire Regiment killed in World War I. There are several similar ones on the chancel screen. Before the west window stands a large bell of uncertain origin, but the tower holds a peal of six, the gift, together with the clock, of Mr. W. Spindler, a wealthy German resident of Old Park, St Lawrence.

V. old Church
2nd oldest

The White Horse Inn

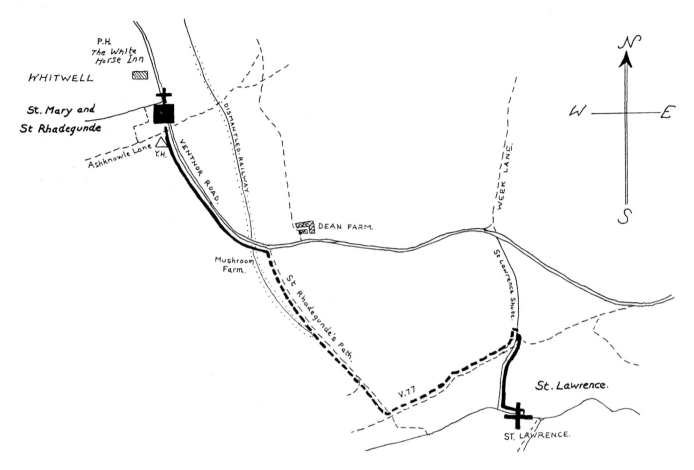

13. ST MARY & ST RHADEGUNDE, Whitwell, to ST LAWRENCE   *1.5 miles*

Leave the Church by turning right and proceeding up the main road for about 0.5 mile. This will bring you to St Rhadegunde's footpath (on your right). Take this, continuing uphill for 0.5 mile. Continue through a field to a sign-post about 100 yards away. Take the left path (V77), continuing uphill and over a stile. Continue along the edge of the field until you come to the end of it. Continue around it keeping the edge to you right. After 100 yards there are steps and a stile on your right. Cross the stile and continue down more steps to the road. Turn right, down a very steep hill (St Lawrence Shute). At the end of this turn left and proceed to St Lawrence Church in about 100 yards to your right.

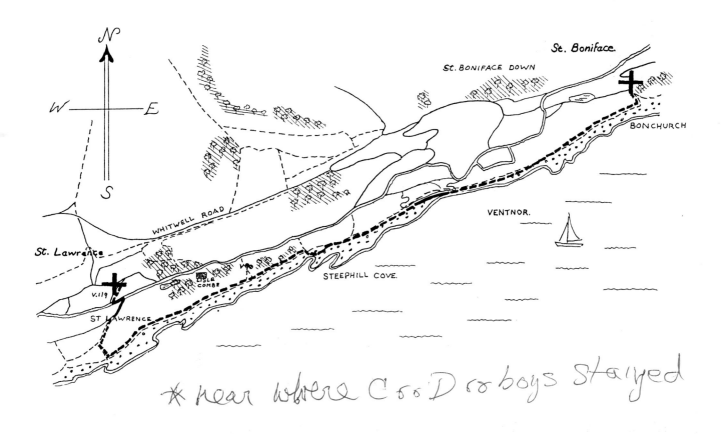

near where CooDooboys stayed

14. ST LAWRENCE to ST BONIFACE, Bonchurch   *3.5 miles*

Take footpath (V119) downhill to the main road. Turn left and cross over, taking the first turning right (Woolverton Road) for 150 yards. You'll see a footpath on your left to Woody Bay. Take the next footpath on the left which leads to the cliff edge. Turn left, reaching Lisle Combe in a quarter of a mile. Take Footpath V90 to Steephill Cove. This will climb again to the cliff edge. Continue along this, past Ventnor and take the new FP along the shore to Bonchurch. When the path ends look for the way up by houses to the Church.

St Lawrence

The church of St Lawrence has given its name to the hamlet nearby. St Lawrence was a martyr who was roasted on a grid-iron during the persecution of Christians by the Emperor Valerian, but he has no particular connection with the Island.

It's almost certain that this little church began its life as a manorial chapel of the de Aula family who held the manor of Wolverton-under-Wath (Stream), and they named it after their patron saint.

Originally the church was the smallest in England measuring a mere 20 x 11 feet. Despite this, it was raised to the status of a parish church in 1305. Thus it stayed for centuries and it was not until 1842 that the present chancel was added; this is slightly higher than the nave which has resulted in several old table tombs being partially buried.

The original piscina (a sink for the rinsing of the chalice) is still in the south wall. In the wall opposite is a small window through which the Sanctus bell used to be rung during Mass or the Communion Service. Also in the north wall is a small blocked-up doorway which used to be the entrance. It was walled-up in 1754 when the Rector, hurrying in for a service, struck his head upon the low lintel, sustaining injuries from which he died.

The porch over the south door was added early last century by the Hon. C. A. Pelham who had inherited through marriage the wealth and property of Sir Richard Worsley, following his death in 1805, there being no male heir. This is the gentleman who, as a mark of gratitude, had the huge memorial to Sir Richard (known locally as 'the bath') erected in the church at Godshill.

The bell you see inside mounted on a special housing is said to have come from the Priory of Appuldurcombe before it was dissolved in 1414 by Henry V.

When the Victorians considered enlarging the church to accommodate more people, it was thought more expedient to build a completely new church. This was designed by Sir Giles Gilbert Scott, the designer of the Albert Memorial. The new church is a classic example of Victorian Gothic architecture. It contains some splendid pre-Raphaelite stained glass which was salvaged when a famous hospital in Ventnor was closed.

A view from above St Lawrence

St Boniface, Bonchurch

There was probably a church on this site in Saxon times, dedicated to St Boniface who was a monk from Devon, eventually martyred in Holland in 755. By the time of the Norman Conquest, there was little more than a ruin here, and legend has it that it was rebuilt by monks from the Abbey of Lyre in Normandy. Certainly nearby is a small indentation of coast which is known as Monks Bay.

The church is the second smallest on the Island (the smallest being St Lawrence); it measures a mere 48 feet by 12 feet, and seats eighty people in the nave, two galleries having long since been demolished. This century has seen considerable alterations which have detracted from its medieval character. Nevertheless, its smallness and surrounding trees and lush vegetation, interlaced by a stream and several small water falls, all continue to maintain its charrn.

Inside there are a few memorial tablets, but these are Victorian; one is to a young surgeon from Essex who died in March 1811. How his remains come to be in a vault in the churchyard is a mystery.

Notice the 13th century window in the west wall, and the box tombs with indecipherable inscriptions, but obviously centuries old. Mention must be made of the many literary celebrities who have visited this spot, and some of whom lived nearby. These include Macaulay, Alfred Noyes, H. de Vere Stacpoole, Keats, Dickens and the poet Algernon Swinburne, who is buried here.

Lisle Combe

N.B. The new church at St Boniface was built in 1848 to accommodate the increasing population in the vicinity. It is large and gloomy, but this has the advantage of enhancing the beauty of the stained glass windows.

Steephill Cove

On leaving the Church, go downhill along a narrow alley on the left, to nearby East Dene. Bear left until you reach an attractive old cottage where you join the Coastal Footpath (FP167) This path takes you over newly-made wooden steps and walkways, and passing two tea-gardens en route. You eventually emerge on to a narrow road where you can see Culver Cliff. Descend about half a mile then take the first road on your left (Priory Road), which is opposite the site of the old hospital. Continue for about 150 yards and take Footpath 91 on your left to the Old Village Church. The footpath comes out on the main road opposite the Church.

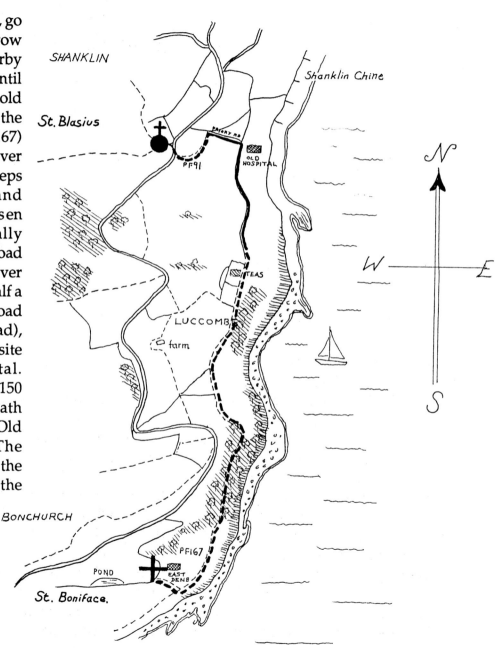

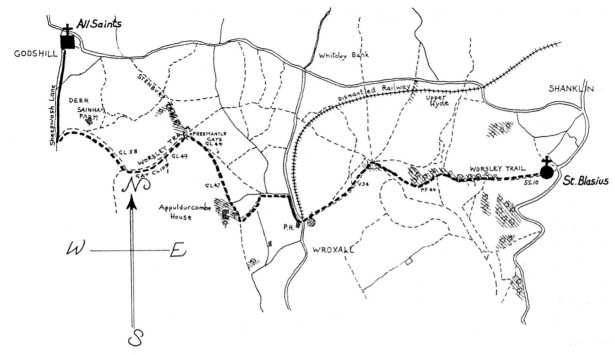

16. ST BLASIUS, Shanklin, to ALL SAINTS, Godshill   5 miles

On leaving the Church, take FP SS10 at the top of the churchyard. This will take you uphill through two fields. Then climb two flights of steps and two stiles with rough terrain between them. Continue straight ahead about 500 yards, ignoring the stile on the right; but 30 yards ahead there is another stile where you join FP 44 which is partially hidden by a tree. Keep straight on and where five footpaths meet, turn left down V34. Continue to farm gate with Appuldurcombe House in the distance. Turn left down a narrow track and through a gate to the road. Continue to Castle Road where you can see Wroxall Church. At the bottom of the road turn right into main road for 300 yards then turn left to Appuldurcombe House. Bear left opposite GL44 until you reach the black railings of Appuldurcombe House, then turn right. Continue uphill until you reach the entrance to the House. Cross the stile opposite and continue up Footpath GL47. Rejoin GL44 about 100 yards from Freemantle Gate, go through gate and turn left in a few yards up GL49. Continue up with a stone wall on your left with Gat Cliff above. Pass through the gate at the end of the stone wall. Turn right along Footpath GL58. On reaching Sainham Farm (where there is a herd of deer) turn left. Continue to the end of the path then turn right into Sheepwash Lane. Proceed along this until you reach the Church.

St Blasius, Shanklin

It is hard to believe that the church one sees today has derived from the simple place of worship which existed here for centuries. From a print of 1794, we know that there was merely a rectangular nave with a bellcote at the west end and a porch entrance in the south wall. It was like that for another 58 years when a complete re-build and extension was begun. Today it must be conceded that the Victorians produced a church of unique shape and considerable appeal.

The simple church began its life as a private chapel for the Norman lords of Shanklin Manor. They had adopted the name "de Insula". (This ultimately became Lisle, and this family became one of the wealthiest and most influential on the Island.)

The early building was dedicated to John the Baptist. Why it was changed in modern times is not clear; we only know that St Blasius was connected with a chantry in the 14th century.

Inside the present church, look for the piscina and the sedile (priest's seat) set into a wall, each framed in matching and decorative wooden panelling; but as the floor has now been raised, the sedile is obviously no longer usable. This raising of the floor has also partly hidden several black sepulchral slabs to the memory of several members of the Popham family who were Lords of the Manor in the 18th century.

In the centre of the sanctuary are slabs commemorating three Popham children, and in the chancel wall is a most attractive tablet to another described as "a most excellent child".

In the south transept are two small stained glass windows in memory of two other young people. An interesting treasure is an early 16th century chest beautifully carved in oak; then there is the pulpit which has five carved panels. They are probably 17th century and of German or Flemish origin. The south transept has a pair of painted boards showing the initials of Charles I and Charles II. These were common at the time of the Stuarts but most were destroyed in 1649. The two doubtless owe their preservation to being hidden by some Royalist supporter.

East Dene

All Saints, Godshill

This is one of the most popular churches in England as far as the number of visitors is concerned. The present church is the fourth to be built on this hill site, formerly a pagan shrine; the first church was erected in the 11th century.

Be sure to note a most unusual mural in the south transept. It shows Christ crucified on a flowering lily with three branches. It was discovered only in the last century when the whitewash of reformers began to peel off. This Lily Cross is unique to this church. The magnificent tomb of Caen Stone is that of Sir John Leigh and his wife Agnes. The effigies are of alabaster and are worthy of the wealthiest people on the Island at that time. Sir John's feet rest on a representation of a wild boar which is said to have been instrumental in his death by causing his horse to rear.

This couple's daughter Anne married James Worsley, a Lancastrian. They inherited the Manor of Appuldurcombe (two miles away) and founded the Island's most important family. James had been a page at the court of Henry VII and then a "whipping boy" for Prince Hal. Later he was to be well rewarded for this doubtful honour, for when Prince Hal became Henry VIII, Richard was knighted and made Captain of the Isle of Wight. His son, another Richard, was entrusted with the building of forts at Cowes, East Cowes, Sandown and Yarmouth - the last after the catastrophic loss of the *Mary Rose*. He also caused a cannon to be installed in every parish, usually in the church. He and his two sons, killed in a gunpowder accident, are remembered in the monument to the right of the High Altar.

Several other Worsleys are remembered here, in particular Richard (d. 1805) by a 30 ton sarcophagus! This was erected by the husband of his niece, Henrietta Simpson, who inherited the Worsley fortune.

Search out the remains of stairs to the medieval Rood loft, and note the bell-cote outside the south transept. In addition, there is the usual parish chest with three locks, some beautiful stained glass windows, and the base of a 15th century preaching cross which is mounted with a sun dial; it lies to the left of the south porch.

Appuldurcombe Manor

17. ALL SAINTS, Godshill, to ST GEORGE, Arreton   *4 miles*

Leave Godshill Church and turn right, via the beautiful old cottages and downhill into the main road. Turn right in about 150 yards and take the footpath on your left. Reaching the car park, cross it and go over a stile. Continue for about 350 yards, then turn left and follow a track past Moor Farm. Proceed straight on for about 1000 yards then bear left. You will pass Great Budbridge Manor, then turn right passing Little Budridge Farm into East Lane and continue along. Turn right on to a track to Perreton Farm. Bearing left through the farm, go through a wide green gate and a second gate. Turn left over a stile and cross a field. At the end of the field turn right for 50 yards, then left over another stile for about 150 yards. You will see another stile on the skyline slightly to your left. Ascend a steep bank and cross this stile. Continue ahead for a third of a mile until you come to the main road. Turn left, then right when you reach the White horse P.H. St George's Church Arreton lies before you uphill.

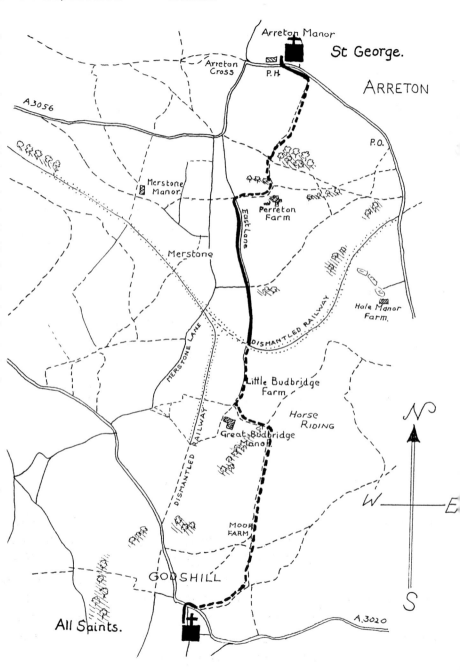

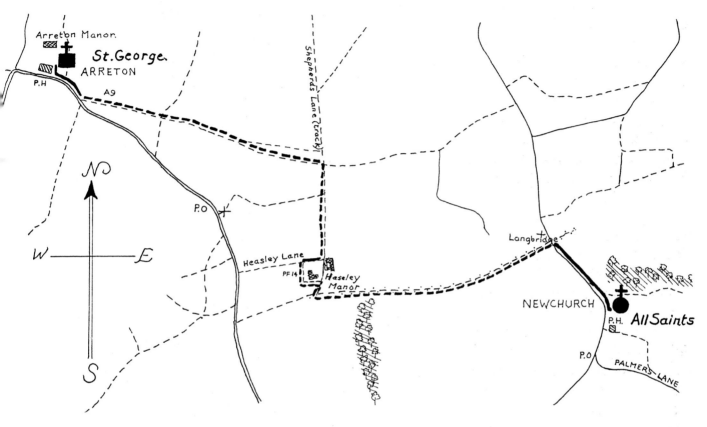

18. ST GEORGE, Arreton, to ALL SAINTS, Newchurch   *2.5 miles*

On leaving St George's, turn left into the main road and continue for about 100 yards; then turn left into Bridleway A9 (Mersley). Go straight on past sign-posts, then turn right into a bridleway. Ignoring the sign-post 30 yards on, carry straight on, turn right into a narrow road at Haseley Manor. Turn left past the car park (FP14). Cross over the bridge across a stream and turn left after a stile. After about 100 yards turn right the far side of Haseley Manor. After about 100 yards turn left (Langbridge). Carry on, with the stream on your right (an old railway track). In about two-thirds of a mile the track comes out on to the main road where you turn right uphill. Newchurch is about 300 yards ahead.

St George, Arreton

V. Vivian

This church still shows some remains of Saxon workmanship, but mostly the present building is thought to date from the 11th century.

It used to be administered by Quarr Abbey monks, and this continued until the dissolution of the monasteries under Henry VIII. The huge buttresses supporting the tower (late 13th century) were added two centuries later when indications of subsidence caused alarm. The addition of the tower made the west wall an internal one, causing the Saxon doorway and window to be well preserved. The same applies to a small stained glass depiction of the Crucifixion. Naturally the structure has undergone many alterations and additions. Keen observers will notice that the edges of the tower have been chamferred to permit entrance of light from two lancet windows.

Inside is a memorial brass to Harry Hawles of Hale Manor who is said to have fought at Agincourt. In 1648 the church register records the burial of three corpses found in the snow. An interesting headstone is that of Elizabeth Wallbridge who became the heroine of a 19th century "best seller" *The Dairyman's Daughter*, included in the Rev. L. Richmond's *Annals of the Poor*. Visitors should note the parish chest which has three locks. Two wardens and the vicar each held a different key and had to operate them together to preclude anyone being dishonest.

The cover of the font was elaborately carved by a woman; and some of the panels of the pulpit

Freemantle Gate

came from a cottage cabinet purchased by the Island architect Percy Stone, who designed the structure.

High in the north wall of the chancel is a tablet to William Culnet of Combley, said to have been distantly related to the last Emperor of Constantinople. There are several other interesting memorial brasses, and on the west wall hang two bequest boards. Space forbids details of numerous other interesting characters who contributed to the life of the area.

Great Budbridge Manor

All Saints, Newchurch

V. Vivian

The weather-boarding around the steeple makes this church unique among Island churches. Among the traces of Norman building inside are three lancet windows on the north side of the chancel. Originally there was no glass, and they were closed by shutters.

This church was another of the six given to the Abbey of Lyre in Normandy by William Fitz-osbern shortly after the Conquest. Subsequently French monks built the north and south aisles in the 12th century. Early in the 15th century, when the church was "bought" back by the Abbey of Beaulieu, the tower was added on the south porch.

It was not until the 18th century that the wooden cladding was added. This was an unusual development, and one ponders the reason. The English monks soon set to work on a rood screen and loft. Traces of them are still visible though they were removed early last century.

High in the west wall is a 14th century rose window. The pulpit is an 18th century pannelled one, and there is a gilded lectern. Decide for yourself whether it takes the form of a pelican or an eagle. Still preserved is a 19th century barrel organ with a repertoire of five hymns in case an organist was not forthcoming. There is also an early 18th century Bible with a printing error - giving the Parable of the Vinegar for Vineyard!

It is quickly obvious from the barren appearance of the churchyard that the headstones have been re-sited along the walls - presumably a labour-saving idea. The ancient sun dial standing in the centre of the grass was a gift from George Maurice Bisset who had it removed from his manor lawns at Knighton Gorges. This gentleman was associated with the infamous Hellfire Club; he also eloped with Lady Worsley, the wife of Sir Richard Worsley of Appuldurcombe. The consequent scandal ruined the latter's career and he moved to the mainland. Years later, Bisset had his stately house demolished brick by brick, as he lay dying (sheltering in a gardener's cottage), rather than have it fall into the hands of a disobedient daughter. He seems to have been "quite a character".

Haseley Manor

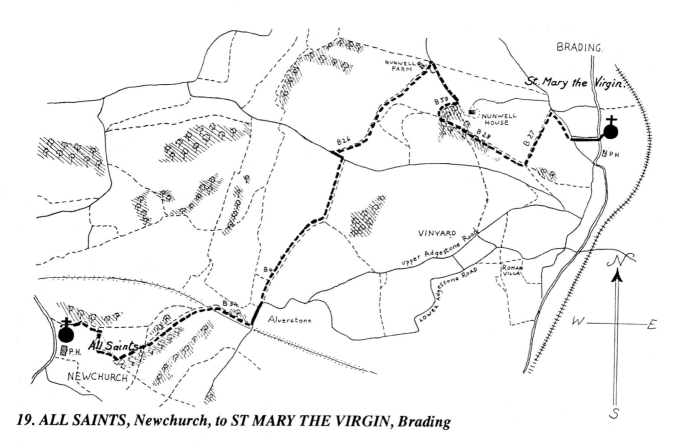

19. ALL SAINTS, Newchurch, to ST MARY THE VIRGIN, Brading

Outside the Church, turn right through the churchyard and over a stile in the wall in the far corner, next to the cemetery. Turn right and proceed along a track for about 300 yards till you come to a sign (PF N12 Borthwood); about 150 yards past this sign, turn right across the field to the bottom.

Proceed straight along a narrow unmarked footpath for about 40 yards. Cross the stream and stile and carry straight on uphill for about 30 yards, bearing left, then turn left over grass for about 250 yards. Cross a stile and follow the path up through a copse.

Reaching a signpost, turn LEFT (not right) and cross another stile. Descend through the middle of the field, approx. 150 yards, pass through a hedge and follow path through a copse for about 30 yards. Cross a bridge on to a wide path. Opposite is a sign B54 (Alverstone).

Take this path and carry on with a stream on your left. Cross a wide concrete bridge, then a stile and into a road. Turn left and contine straight on for about 100 yards where the road bears to the right, on to a lane (no through road).

Where this bears left, go straight on, Bridleway B4. Continue on this, passing a stile on your right. Keep on going up.

Eventually turn left into the main road and turn right after 80 yards on to footpath B26. Keep on, down the field, then turn left through a gate to a grassy path.

Pass through another gate and straight on through a farm. Just past this, turn right uphill on a narrow track to Nunwell House rear entrance. Turn right up Bridleway B59, then through a gate on to Bridleway B28 and turn left. After about half a mile take a left fork for about 50 yards.

Turn left down FP B27, then right at lane before main road. At the end of this lane turn left into the road. Brading Church lies at the end.

20. ST MARY THE VIRGIN, Brading to ST JOHN THE BAPTIST, Yaverland   1.25 miles

Turn left into Quay Lane and continue over a railway bridge. This lane becomes a track, and at the end of the track pick up FP B3. Follow this over the River Yar Bridge - two in fact - and after 15 yards take a right fork over a stile. Go straight through the field and over a hill. Cross another stile to the centre of a field and on to a gate which opens onto the main road. Directly opposite you will find the road to Yaverland, and the Church is about 200 yards further on - on the left.

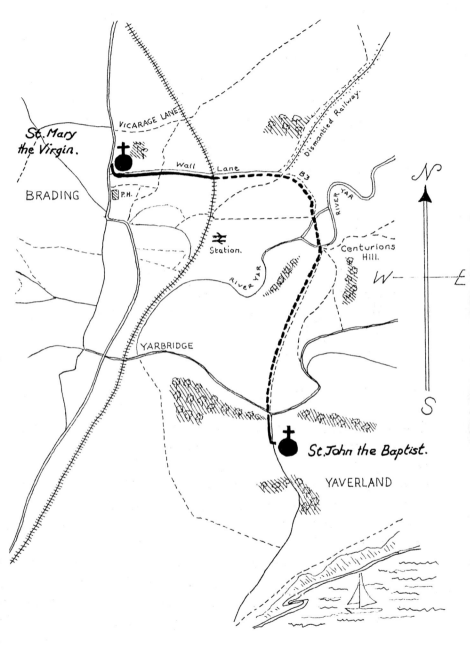

St Mary the Virgin, Brading

Although, unaccountably, there is no mention of this church in the Domesday Book, there is no doubt that a church was here several hundred years before. The oldest parts of the nave go back to the 12th century, the tower to the 13th, the chancel with its chapels to the 14th, and continuing development for the next two centuries.

The tower is unusual, being built on piers, and open on three sides, the fourth accommodating the west door into the church. The chancel is dominated by an ornate altar and a carved reredos.

On the north side is a chapel built in the 14th century and dedicated to the de Alva family. On the south side is the Oglander chapel. This family came over with the Conqueror and settled in Nunwell. It has been a powerful force in this portion of the island for 800 years.

A three-light window on the south wall depicts the story of the Prodigal Son. Another, installed in 1888 by Emilia Scott in memory of her family, shows the Crucifixion in the centre light, and on one side the three Marys and on the other, two disciples. In the west wall of the south side is a four-light window showing eight incidents in the life of Christ.

The 13th century font is worth noting, also two old chests, four hatchments, and, in the belfry, a peal of eight bells.

To return to the Oglander family; its members intermarried with a number of the great families on the Island, and even with royalty. The consequent influx of wealth has led to Nunwell being one of the island's show-pieces.

Perhaps the most well-known member of the family is Sir John Oglander (born 1585) who was the Deputy Governor of the Island and a friend of Charles I. In consequence he suffered fines and imprisonment under the Commonwealth. There are three ornate box tombs for his grandfather Oliver, his father William and himself. There is much else of interest here, but space forbids going into further details.

Nunwell House

St John the Baptist, Yaverland

Built about the middle of the 12th century, St John the Baptist Church at Yaverland, like so many others, began as the private chapel of a wealthy Norman family - the de Aulas who owned the Manor of Yaverland.

It consists of a nave and chancel, separated by a typical Norman arch, probably the best of its type on the Island. Another such is seen over the entrance door and this is now protected by a porch, so it should continue to maintain its excellent condition. The chapel was raised to the status of a parish church in the 15th century, but it retained its links with the mother church at Brading. Indeed, it was compelled to supply a certain quantity of candles for lighting, straw (for floor covering?) and a sum of money.

The altar today is a simple one, but it is backed by a delicately carved alabaster reredos, depicting the four Evangelists and many other saints. There is a good deal of stained glass, though none of this is ancient. The south wall of the chancel has a pair of two-light windows depicting Charity, Faith, Love and Humility. The one over the altar has three lights depicting scenes from the life of Christ, the centre one, naturally, being the Crucifixion.

Notice that a wall between the nave and chancel has two openings. One contains the remnants of steps leading to a rood loft; the other, known as a "Squint", gives a view of the high altar from the corner of the nave which is thought to have been the site of the Chantry chapel existing in 1305; but no trace of this has survived apart from a window and an early English arch.

The church as we find it today owes its appearance to extensive restoration in 1889, so there is a strong Victorian appearance about it. Even so, something of its medieval charm still survives.

The River Yar

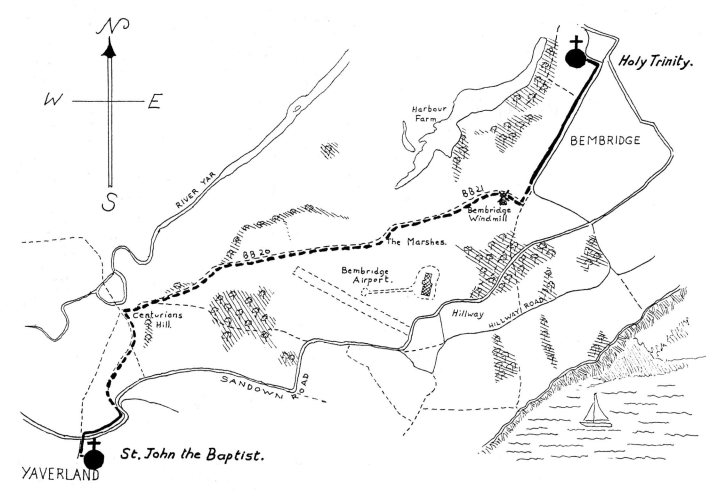

21. ST JOHN THE BAPTIST, Yaverland, to HOLY TRINITY, Bembridge   3 miles

Leave the Church by taking a right turn up the hill, then turn right into the main road. Continue for about 250 yards. Just past the left-hand bend there is an unmarked path on the left. Take this; you will find it bears round to the right along the edge of the field, with a hedge and a fence on your right. In about 700 yards cross a stile and turn right, continuing to sign-posts. Take the left path (BB20) and continue through the middle of fields, crossing several stiles. You'll see Bembridge Airport on your right. Follow signposts all the way. This becomes BB21 on your left uphill to Bembridge Windmill; cross a stile and turn left and you will come out on to a road. Continue straight ahead and the Church is just past a left-hand bend.

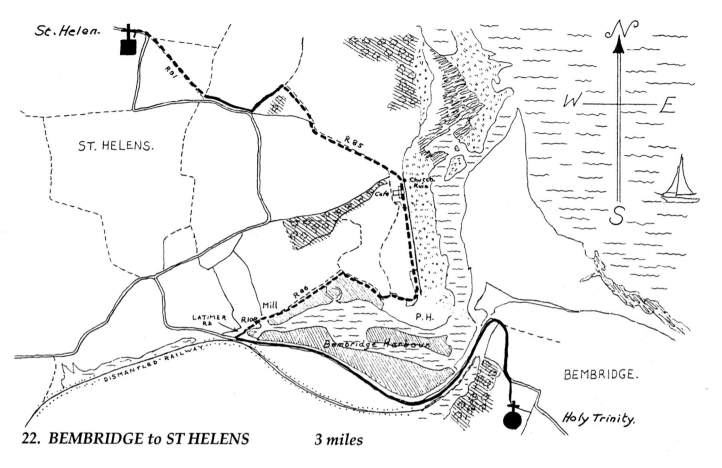

22. BEMBRIDGE to ST HELENS   *3 miles*

Leave Holy Trinity by turning left down Church Road. Turn left at the junction and proceed to Bembridge Harbour. Walk round this, noticing the house-boats en route. Take the first right (Latimer Road). Continue on FP R108 (50 yards) then pick up the Coastal Path (R86) which is, in fact, the Causeway. This crossed, turn right, then left just before some buildings, then turn left again which will take you to the Front. Walk along the Duver, noticing the old railway carriages used as bathing-huts. When you reach the ruins of the old church, take the road immediately opposite on your left. This road bends round to the right as you take the Coastal Path (R85). Keep the hedge to your right. Cross the stile on your right and go uphill to a narrow road. Turn left into this. At its end, turn right when reaching the main road. After about 250 yards, take the footpath on your right (R81). Cross the centre of the field and go through the gate at the end, and you will find St Helen's Church is opposite.

Holy Trinity, Bembridge

Unlike most Island churches, this is a comparative newcomer. It began life as a Chapel of Ease (with a surrounding burial ground) in 1827, being consecrated on August 16th. The simple rectangular building with its tower and spire thus became the parish church of the recently-established parish of Bembridge.

Funds for its erection came from subscriptions, also from Trinity House since the steeple was to serve as an additional sea-mark. By 1844, however, the building became something of a menace to worshippers. Whether this was due to the use of the Bembridge Ledge Limestone, the durability of which is suspect, or because the foundations were built on blue slipper clay, is not clear. Anyway, by dint of amazing enterprise and generosity, a new building was erected in the vicinity, but well clear of the treacherous blue slipper. This building was consecrated in July 1846, and dedicated to the Holy Trinity.

Its appearance and structure was obviously inspired by that of its medieval forebear viz the parish church of St Mary's in Brading, and obviously it is much larger than the original Chapel of Rest.

In 1896 an organ chamber and vestry were added. The excellent Foster and Adams organ in use today has replaced several more modest predecessors, and as recently as 1984 was rebuilt and several stops revised. In 1982 a side chapel was added in the south aisle.

It is not known when the carved reredos was installed, but the figures of the two apostles, Peter and Paul, were added in 1932 as a memorial to a former vicar, the Rev. Gwennap Moore, MA, DSO, who served from 1926 to 1930.

The spire carries a cross which has replaced the original weather vane, and the steeple contains three bells installed in 1865. These are operated by levers, and the simple "doh ray me" arrangement permits a surprising number of pleasing variations.

Bembridge Windmill

St Helens

The present St. Helens Church (a re-building) dates back to 1830-31 (the Chancel to 1862). Some of the floor slabs in the north and south transepts appear to be grave-stones from a former church burial ground on the Duver; the oldest dates back to 1707.

Religious activity first began in this area when Bishop Wilfred landed at Brading Haven in 704 A.D. He had journeyed from Chichester. Shortly afterwards, Hildila his chaplain, built a wooden church on the Duver. This structure was probably burned down by the Danes when they invaded the Island in 998 in the reign of Ethelred (the Unready).

Early in the 12th century the Priory at St Helens was occupied by Cluniac monks who built a church in stone thus making good the destruction of Hildila's church. It was named after the mother of the Roman emperor, Constantine, who had championed Christianity and formally embraced it on his deathbed. The Prior, Robert, probably built the tower, much of which remains.

During Henry V's reign, alien monastic orders were suppressed, and in 1467, Edward IV granted the land to Eton College; during the following two centuries the church fell into a disgraceful state of ruin. In 1656, Cromwell's Commissioners recommended that the structure be pulled down before it fell, and a church built in the centre of the Parish. However, nothing was done, and deterioration continued and it fell into the sea, with the exception of the tower which was re-inforced and revised and used as a sea-mark.

After a wait of more than 60 years, a church on the site of the present one was completed by 1719 during the reign of George I. This was re-built as stated above between 1830-31.

The remains of St Helen's Church

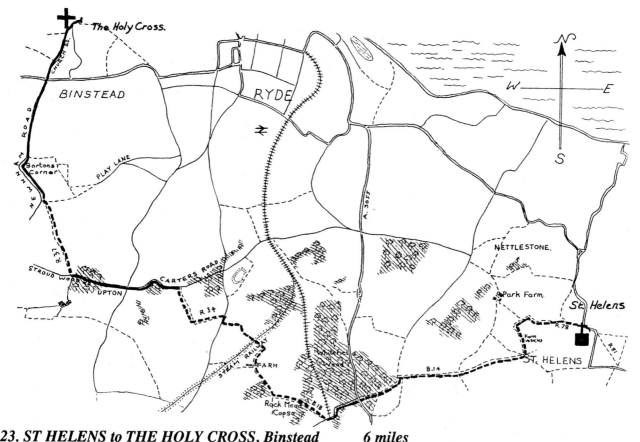

23. ST HELENS to THE HOLY CROSS, Binstead   6 miles

On leaving the church, turn left for about 100 yards and (on a right-hand bend) take the bridle path (R78) on your left. Pass through a gate, turn left and continue bearing left uphill about 300 yards (passing several old farm vehicles on the way). When at the top you will find 3 paths with gates. Go through to grassy path on your right. Continue with a hedge on your left for about 600 yards, then take B14 (keep the hedge to your right) to the end of the field. Pass through a gateway and a wooded area for about 300 yards

then take the second turning on your left. (They are about 50 yards apart.) Continue down a track to the main road, when you take the road opposite (Harding Shute). Cross the railway bridge and after about 100 yards take FP B18 on your right through a copse diagonally and across a field. At its end turn right onto a bridle path. After about 0.25 mile you will come to Whitefield Farm. Go through this and turn to your right on to a bridle path. Make for a signal which is part of the Haven Street Steam Railway. Cross the railway

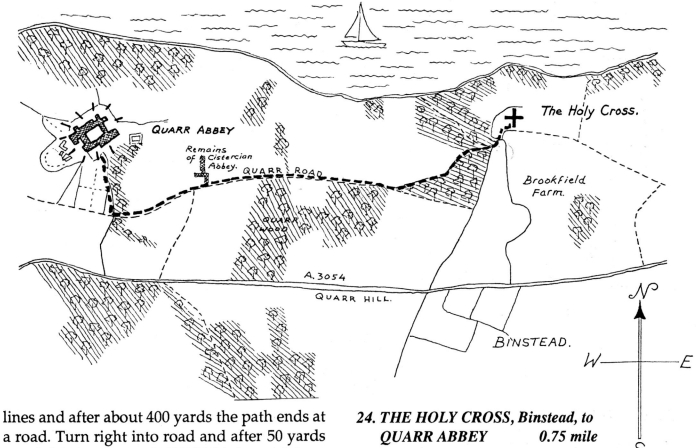

QUARR ABBEY

Remains of Cistercian Abbey.

QUARR ROAD

QUARR WOOD

The Holy Cross.

Brookfield Farm.

A.3054
QUARR HILL.

BINSTEAD.

N
W — E
S

lines and after about 400 yards the path ends at a road. Turn right into road and after 50 yards turn left into a footpath (R34); this bears right at the bottom (about 300 yards) and after a similar distance turn left into Carters Road. Straight on at the roundabout and in about 700 yards turn right at a farm, following footpath R37 for about another 700 yards. Then turn right into Newnham Road. Continue on this for nearly 0.75 mile when you will come to the main road. Here you take the road opposite (Church Road) and you will arrive at Binstead Church after about one third of a mile.

24. THE HOLY CROSS, Binstead, to QUARR ABBEY   0.75 mile

Come out of the Church, and in about 50 yards turn right into Church Road. Proceed along this about 30 yards, then turn right again into Bridleway. Keep to this for about a quarter of a mile then turn right again, continuing for about half a mile, when you will reach cross-roads, from where you will see Quarr Abbey on your right.

The Holy Cross, Binstead

V. Vivian

Most of the building was erected in 1844, and the bellcote at the west end in 1925. The bell itself is thought to have come from Quarr when the Abbey closed in the early 16th century.

The exact date of the original church on this site is in some doubt. It may be pre-Norman or it may be early 12th century when Quarr Abbey was built. The oldest surviving part is the chancel (13th century or before). You will find some early herring-bone masonry in the walls, and on the south side is a square window from which the Mass and Sanctus bell was rung in the days when the window could be opened.

In the churchyard (largely cleared now and the headstones lining the walls) is a table tomb belonging to a previous rector - Parson James Goodlad, an apt name if ever there was one - who died in 1620. Nearby is a medieval "scratch" sun-dial. You will also find a double headstone with an interesting, though sad, story. It relates how Thomas Sivell, a ferryman, was shot by Customs & Excise men who had mistaken him for a smuggler. Poor John was 61, and he met his death on June 15, 1786. His wife lies alongside.

Moving over to the north side, you will find the grave of one Samuel Landon who must have been something of a giant, for he is said to have been "the biggest man in the world". He died in 1844.

The oldest item here is the Norman archway in the south wall of the churchyard. In earlier times, this was the north door to the church, but it was re-sited during the rebuilding operations of 1864. The grotesque stone figure at the apex deserves special notice. Locals call it The Idol, but experts think it is a pagan sculpture with protective and fertility connotations.

Inside there is a magnificent Victorian font and a beautifully carved and elaborate Rector's stall. Note the ancient window now filled with very modern stained glass which some might feel was a trifle misplaced; also the hammer beam roof put in by local craftsmen following a serious fire in 1969. The reconstruction at that time permitted sliding doors to be fitted under the gallery, thus allowing part of the church to be used for secular meetings and social purposes. Truly an innovation in a church of this type.

Stroud Wood Road, Upton

Quarr Abbey (near Ryde)

The old Abbey, surviving now only as a ruin, was suppressed along with so many others in 1536 by edict of Henry VIII. It was then called the Abbey of our Lady of the Quarry, because nearby there had been a shallow seam of stone which was soon exhausted by the digging of a series of pits. (In Dorset, the word quarr is still used for an outcrop of stone in a field.)

The modern Abbey was founded in 1908. It came into existence through the drive and initiative of a French Abbott - Dom Paul Delatte - who first installed 100 monks in Appuldurcombe House as an initial base. Later, 20 of them were transferred to Quarr Abbey House, a venerable old property, purchased in May 1907 from Lt Thomas B. H. Cochrane, the Deputy Governor of the Wight.

An architect from a French monastery was then commissioned to draw up the plans for a full scale monastery along Benedictine lines.

Contrary to popular belief, this vast, elaborate building was constructed by an Island firm using some 300 local men who were more accustomed to building houses. However, they worked faithfully and well, and their work still wins acclaim. It was completed just prior to the outbreak of World War I. Its first guest was the French philosopher, Jacques Maritain. During the war, the guest-house was used for the convalescence of wounded soldiers, among whom was the writer and poet Robert Graves.

It was only in 1937 that Quarr was raised to the status of Abbey. It is now an English speaking community, and the two dozen or so inmates follow the community monastic way of life, i.e. prayer, worship, study, farm work and gardening.

Remains of Cistercian Abbey

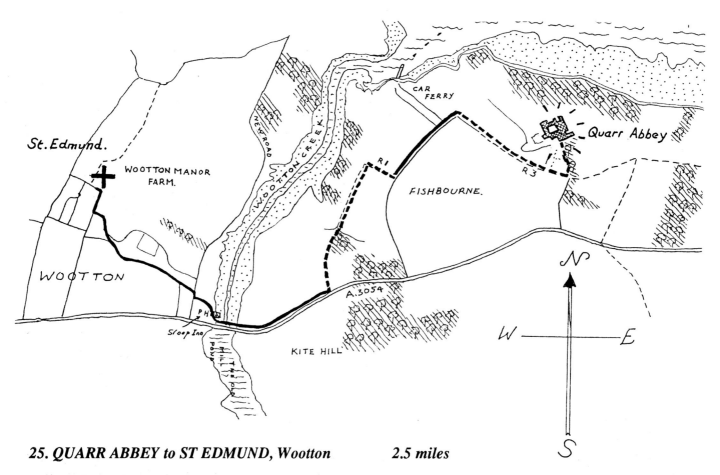

25. QUARR ABBEY to ST EDMUND, Wootton   *2.5 miles*

On leaving the Abbey, retrace your footsteps up the land, and in about 150 yards take a right turn into PF R3. Continue along this for about half a mile then turn left into main road, passing the Fishbourne Ferry; after about 200 yards turn right down PF R1 for 100 yards, then turn left. When the track turns left you will see a driveway on the right. Ignore this but carry straight on through a plantation. You will eventually reach the main road. Turn right and cross a bridge (Old Mill Pond on your left). Just past the Sloop Inn (on your right) take the Coastal FP N190. Go up New Road and turn right at the end of Pump Lane, then left into St Edmund's Walk. At the end of this winding road, turn right into Church Road, and you will find St Edmund's Church on the next corner.

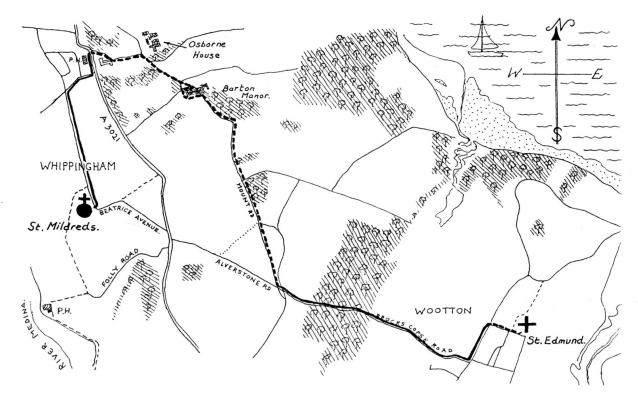

26. ST EDMUND, Wootton, to ST MILDRED'S, Whippingham   3.5 miles

On leaving St Edmund's Church, turn right and at the end of Church Road, turn left. After about 300 yards turn right down Brocks Copse Road, and after 0.75 mile turn right up a track (Mount Road). It's worth looking at the house on the left, in about 600 yards. Continue to the small Manor House on your right, and turn right just past this. Walk towards Barton Manor and look out for an interesting piece of statuary carved out of the bowl of a tree stump. The carving is about 18 feet high and is a very fine piece of work. Go up the path to the left and through a gate by a public phone box. You will soon arrive at Osborne House, once the home of Queen Victoria. Turn left here and then right which will take you to the main road, with the Prince of Wales public house just opposite. Turn left and after about 150 yards turn right down Crossways Road. At the end of this turn left into Beatrice Avenue and after about half a mile you will arrive at Whippingham Church.

St Edmund, Wootton

As with many others, this church was originally the private chapel of a manor - a pre-Norman one and belonging to Queen Edith, the wife of Edward the Confessor.

After the Conquest by the Normans, the manor of Wootton, with several others, went to William FitzOsbern, the "brains" behind the successful Norman landings. However, the chapel retained its Saxon dedication. (King Edmund of East Anglia had been martyred by the Danes for refusing to convert to the worship of the Scandinavian God Odin.) In due course, the manor of Wootton (or Odetone) was taken over by the Lisles, one of the Island's wealthiest landowners. They found it easier to worship here than making the long journey along muddy tracks to the parish church at Whippingham. Hence it came to acquire the dignity of a parish church, and began a long series of extensions and restorations, so that today nothing of the Saxon building remains.

The nave is the oldest part of the Norman edifice, dating back to 1087, and the south door, an outstanding example of a chevron ornamental arch, must also be early Norman. Unusually the nave and the chancel, which is a later extension, are the same width, and the latter is almost as long as the nave which seats only about fifty.

On the north side is a small transept which was once a chantry chapel; but this was dissolved at the same time as the monasteries. Preserved here, though, is a board giving the names of the chantry priests from 1305 to 1536.

The church windows are early English; there are three 13th century lancet windows. The smallest has modern glass (1911). On the south side the largest of three windows has two lights depicting St John the Baptist and St Paul, but when vandalism necessitated restoration, the two became transposed.

The rafters of the chancel roof deserve notice. They have been set close together, yet the plaster between them bears an "E" motive, and there is a crown and the arrows of martyrdom. Where the nave ends, there is a massive rood beam bearing a stylised figure of Christ. The font is an unusual shape (one would be forgiven if a garden ornament came to mind; and there is a fine oak Jacobean pulpit.

The Sloop Inn, Wootton

St Mildred's, Whippingham

V. Vivian

As with many Island churches, there has been a sanctuary here since before the Norman Conquest. However, the sole relic of the Saxon building is a wedge-shaped stone bearing a carving depicting horsemen; it is to be seen in the west wall of the present entrance.

An early 19th century water-colour gives some idea of the former structure, though it is safe to assume from our knowledge of the history of other churches, that the subject of the painting also had undergone numerous enlargements and improvements during pre-Victorian centuries.

The building standing in early Norman times, had, along with five other Island churches, been given over to the jurisdiction of the Abbot of Lyre in Normandy, by one of William the Conqueror's chief generals - William FitzOsbern - who had been given the Island as a reward for his military services.

Early last century all the old building was demolished and the renowned architect, John Nash, rebuilt it.

When Queen Victoria built the imposing Osborne House and came to live there frequently, it was thought that the Nash building was hardly appropriate for royal attendance. Consequently a new church was built in 1854, using the east wall of the Nash structure. Then, between 1860-61, the remainder of the building was replaced. The design was that of the Consort, Prince Albert, under the guidance of the architect, A. J. Humbert, who was later to design Sandringham.

The new church was dedicated to St Mildred, an Anglo-Saxon princess who succeeded her mother as Abbess of Minster (the Isle of Thanet) and the communities of St Augustine and St Gregory in Canterbury. It was in the last-named that her remains were interred in 1033.

As the church became increasingly a kind of Royal Chapel, it is not surprising to find that many of the furnishings have been donated by members of the Royal Family. Most of the memorials, also, are to various relations of the Queen. The carved marble reredos was given in memory of Queen Victoria by her son, King Edward VII, and other members of the Royal Family.

Part of the carpet laid in Westminster Abbey for the coronation of the present Queen now furnishes the Sanctuary. The chair on the north side dates from Commonwealth times and was the gift of Princess Louise, one of Victoria's daughters.

Dionysus, The Greek God of Wine, Carved from a tree
Barton Manor, Whippingham

Greek God of Wine

Osborne House

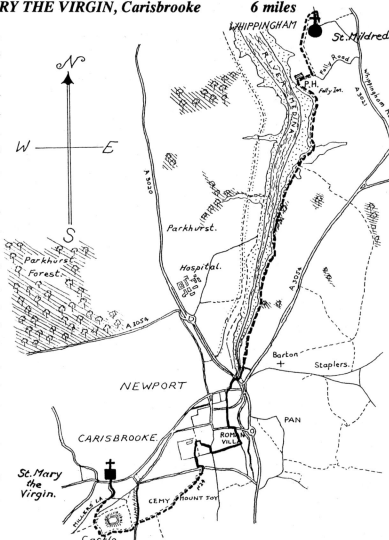

Take a left turn outside Whippingham Church, and at the end of the wall turn left and follow the footpath across fields involving four stiles and going through a copse. You will come out onto a very narrow lane where you turn right and eventually arrive at Folly Inn. Nearby you will find a footpath to your left. Follow this along the banks of the River Medina. On reaching Newport, go under the bridge and turn right into Sea Street. Walk to the end of this then turn left into Holyrood Street. Go through a quaint little lane (Watchbell Lane) and you will come out into the high Street. Cross over and continue straight ahead, going up a pedestrian walkway with St. Thomas' Church on your right. When you reach a corner by God's Providence, cross over and continue straight up Town Lane. This leads to crossroads and traffic lights. Continue straight ahead up Church Litten with Safeways on your left. At the end of Church Litten turn left and cross over into Medina Avenue. Walk on until you find Cypress Road on the right. Go up this, observing the Roman Villa and interesting architecture. At the end of Cypress Road turn right and go downhill for about 100 yards, then to the left (Builders' Centre). Continue with a wire fence to your right. Then take a narrow footpath and find a football field in about 40 yards. Cross this, keeping half-left to the top of the field. Continue straight ahead up Elm Grove. At the end turn left and after about 40 yards, turn right up FP N24 Mount Joy. Go uphill and at the top enjoy several fine views. Continue on past a cemetery and down steps into the road. Take a left turn and after 20 yards turn right onto another footpath.

Pass through a gate after 30 yards and go round to the left of Carisbrooke Castle. Follow the old moat with the Castle on your right until you come to a gate into the car park. Go through this, and 50 yards past the entrance to the Castle, take the footpath leading down steps. Follow this downhill and turn right into Miller's Lane. Cross the stream and up the road to the Church opposite.

28. ST MARY THE VIRGIN, Carisbrooke, to ST JOHN THE BAPTIST, Northwood   5 miles

Follow footpath at the back of Church for about 80 yards and take the righthand turn (PF N60). Continue with playing-field on your left and come out on to road (Wellington Road). Turn left, cross over and take the next road on your right (Hinton Road). Continue to the end (several hundred yards) and turn right into Priors Walk. Opposite is Ward Close; go up this and at the end you will find two paths. Take the path on the right. About 40 yards on, the path ends at a field. Go across the field to your left until you find another footpath on the field's edge. Continue on your right (with the hedge on your left) for about 250 yards, and join wide path with trees on either side. Continue on for about 300 yards when you will see a sign PF N47 Forest Road on your left. Take this and come out at Sycamore Gardens, then turn left for about 100 yards, then right down Maple Drive. Continue on for about 100 yards, where you will see N47 again. Take this on your right (Blackthorn Close), go over footbridge and a stile to a field. Continue straight on up for about 250 yards towards houses when you cross a stile to a road. Turn left into road, cross over and in about 40 yards turn right down a narrow road by a 6'6" sign. At the end turn left into Albany Road, pass a school and in about 200 yards turn right into Whitesmith Road. At its end turn right again for about 80 yards, cross over and go down a path by a bus stop (underpass). This takes you underneath the main road. Turn left and carry on down past I.o.W. College (Dodnor Lane) for about 0.75 mile. Then take cycleway N207 on your left. (This used to be the old Railway Track). Continue for about a mile, until you come to a

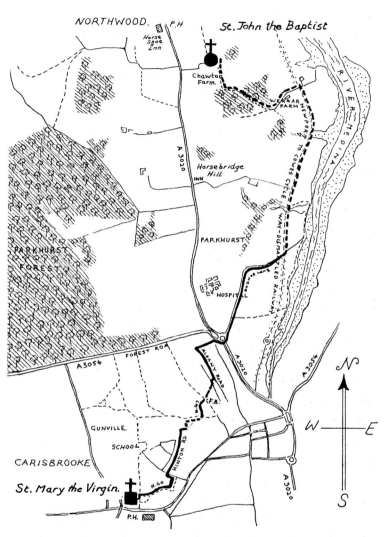

track on your left (Werrar Farm). Turn up here and in about 400 yards turn right into Great Werrar Wood. Follow this path (overgrown in places) uphill and out into a field in about 700 yards. Go straight ahead about 30 yards and then turn right into a track. Continue along this for about 200 yards, then turn left and you will find the Church.

St Mary the Virgin, Carisbrooke

In several places in this book, it is mentioned that shortly after the Norman Conquest the revenues from six Saxon churches were given to the Abbey of Lyre in Normandy, by the first Norman Lord of the Island. For some time no provision was made for the transfer of these dues. Hence the Abbot gained permission to settle a small group of monks on the Island to look after his interests, and a small Priory and Church were established here under the protection of Carisbrooke Castle.

Thus the origins of this church are very different from those of most Island churches, and this is why it is larger than all others barring the Abbey church of Quarr. In addition to the duties mentioned above, the French monks had to carry out their customary duties i.e. visiting the poor and sick, reading and copying manuscripts, etc. Three times a week the leper hospital of St Augustine in the fields near Gunville were visited for the celebration of Mass. There was also manual work associated with the farm and mill to be carried out.

In the reign of Henry V, all alien priories were suppressed in 1414, and put under the control of an English priory at Sheen in Surrey. In the next century, the Carisbrooke Priory was leased to Sir John Leigh of Appuldurcombe, later coming into the hands of the powerful Worsley family, and ultimately, through marriage, to Sir Francis Walsingham, Queen Elizabeth's Secretary of State.

The present church is the sole survivor of the four alien priories on the Island. It is spacious and holds many interesting memorials. One sepulchral slab in the centre aisle of the nave bears a small brass depicting the Arms of William Keeling, the discoverer of the Cocos Islands in the early 17th century. Another is to the memory of Sir Faithful Fortescue, a Royalist officer who, in old age, fled to the Island to escape the plague which was ravaging London. Look for the ancient piscina in the wall of the Lady Chapel.

Carisbrooke Castle

St John the Baptist, Northwood

V. Vivian

This church was built in the second half of the 12th century and was a dependant chapel of the Church at Carisbrooke. It was meant to serve the spiritual needs of people in the northern half of a large parish, in the days when roads were muddy tracks and travelling was difficult. Despite this need, its construction was stretched over an unbelievably long time, and it was not finished, it seems, until early in the next century. After that, no major changes were made until well into the 15th century. This work included the insertion of several more windows. After that, it was not until the middle of last century that, as with so many Island churches, it assumed the appearance we see today.

As a print of 1794 proves, the west end had seen an extraordinary square wooden tower almost as wide as the church, and there was a large dormer window in the south wall of the nave. Naturally, the Victorian restorers, in their desire to make churches look as "Gothic" as possible, quickly had these strange features removed. Certainly, at least as far as the square wooden tower is concerned, the demolition was no great loss.

Inside, all is now conventional, viz. there is a nave flanked by two aisles leading to a small chancel. There are no great tombs and effigies of the illustrious, though there are a few modest memorial tablets and a small amount of stained glass The largest window of three lights was made in 1886, and is to the memory of a devoted wife - Nem Russell of Comforts Farm. There is another large tablet in the south wall, the inscription of which must surely be one of the longest and most comprehensive ever, mentioning some members of a family together with brief mention of some of their exploits.

The original Norman font has survived, although a more modern one is used today. Finally, note the canopied pulpit which is 17th century.

Behind Carisbrooke Church

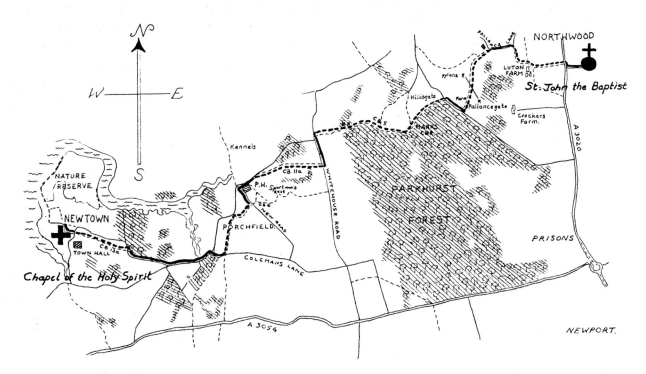

29. ST JOHN THE BAPTIST, Northwood, to CHAPEL OF THE HOLY SPIRIT, Newtown

6 miles

Go down Chawton Lane to the main road. Turn right and in about 20 yards turn left. After about 400 yards go through Luton Farm gate and take the path downhill on your right (this path winds round to your left). Turn left into Pallance Lane. On a bend just before a farm (about 500 yards) turn left (footpath) and after about 100 yards, cross a bridge and stile. Take the left footpath continuing up through the field and under pylon cables. Cross the stile in the corner of the field, pass a farm and emerge onto a road. Turn right here and proceed about 300 yards along the side of Parkhurst Forest. Turn left along a "No

Through Road" for about half a mile when it becomes a Public footpath (CB5). After about another half mile cross a footbridge and a stile at the edge of the forest and continue with a hedge to your left. In about 0.25 mile you will come to a road. Turn left onto the road and continue straight on up Whitehouse Road for about 400 yards. Turn right along FP CB11a for about half a mile. This brings you out at Porchfield. Turn left into the main road and after a further 300 yards you will find the public house Sportsman's Rest, where refreshments are available. Take a left turn along New Road for about 300 yards when you come to a footpath on your right, opposite another footpath (CB6). Take this footpath on your right, continue with hedge to your right for about 250 yards, then cut across to the top right of field. When nearly out to the road, turn sharp left into another footpath for about 500 yards which takes you onto a road. Turn right here and after about 300 yards, turn left into the main road. Continue on this for about half a mile and then turn right (Newtown). Keep to this road for about a third of a mile and, just after a right hand bend, pick up PF CB13a on your left. This runs parallel with the road and after about 700 yards comes out onto a road. Go down the road opposite, and after a right-hand bend you will find the Church ahead of you.

30. CHAPEL OF THE HOLY SPIRIT, *Newtown*, to ST MICHAEL THE ARCHANGEL, *Shalfleet*
1.25 miles

On leaving the Church turn left. When you come to a road, turn right past the old Town Hall. Continue over a bridge and at the end of this road turn right, and immediately to your right you will find a footpath. Take this path and turn left.; it runs parallel to the road. After about 350 yards, you are back on the road. Just past Corfe Farm there is a "No Through Road" sign. Take this by turning to the right. It gets narrower and becomes a winding footpath. In about 100 yards you cross a bridge by Shalfleet Mill. Carry on for 40 yards and turn left to find the New Inn, about 250 yards, on the corner. The Church is virtually opposite.

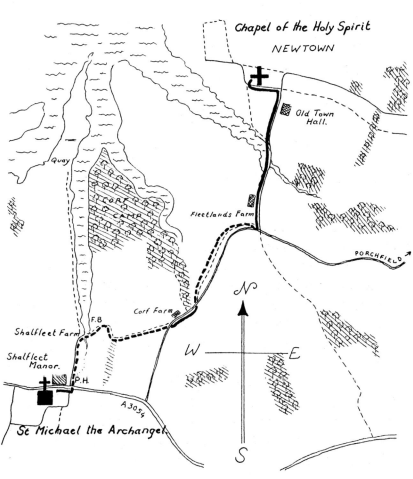

Chapel of the Holy Spirit, Newtown

In August 1377, the town called Newtown, which had been of considerable importance to the Island, was totally destroyed by a French raiding force. In consequence its medieval church was completely ruined.

In 1592 a small Chapel of Ease replaced it, but by 1663 it had fallen into disrepair.

The building you see today dates from 1835; it was raised to the status of Parish Church in 1871. The original dedication was to St Mary Magdalene, but it was later changed to the Holy Ghost. More recently it was changed again to its present dedication.

The church stands between two roads, both dating from medieval times, and one merely a grass track today.

The Sportsman's Rest

St Michael the Archangel, Shalfleet

This church probably began its existence as a private chapel in the days before the Norman Conquest; and as it is mentioned in the Doomsday Book it must have been well established by that time.

The huge squat tower was added in 1070, not to augment the place of worship, but as a place of safety for the villagers whenever French marauders landing in what came to be called Newtown Harbour threatened their lives. For greater safety, no doorway was built into the tower - the frightened villagers had to swarm up a ladder and haul it up after all were inside. They would have had to remember to take with them adequate food and water.

Two centuries later, it was decided to open an entrance into the church from the tower, but this caused cracks to appear and the arch was filled in, and buttresses were added. Last century, the arch was reopened and a small doorway was cut in the tower. This caused a corner to collapse. This century it was discovered that the tower had no foundations, and it was underpinned.

The large south aisle, almost as large as the nave, was added in 1270 to accommodate the villagers. The present chancel goes back to 1290 but the present nave is mainly 19th century. In the 18th century a small cupola was built on top of the tower, but in the beginning of the next century it was replaced with a small steeple which was demolished in 1912. Another feature which has disappeared was the Singing Gallery which came into existence in 1798 at the west end of the south aisle.

On the right of the altar is a 13th century piscina, and the three interesting windows in the south wall are of the same date. Notice the plain circular font, large enough for complete immersion; also the Norman arch which can be seen over the north doorway.

The dedication to St Michael has been operative only since 1964; the earlier dedication had been lost or forgotten, but it was probably a Saxon saint.

The Old Town Hall, Newtown

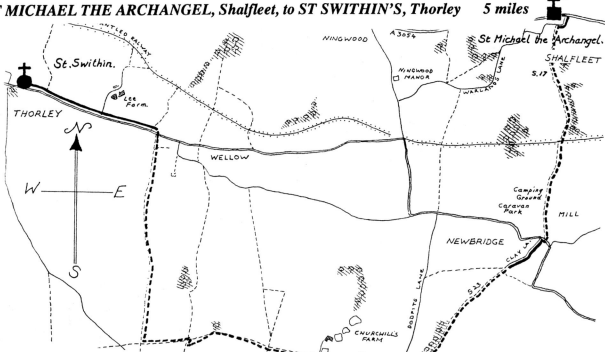

On leaving the Church turn immediately to the right into Church Lane. Opposite the Old Vicarage turn right. Continue for 40 yards then turn left along Footpath S17 (Newbridge). After about 1000 yards, this becomes a bridleway, then a farm track. When this bends to the left, take a footpath and cross a stile. (A mill lies to your left.) On reaching a road turn right and go uphill for 30 yards. Then turn left up Clay Lane. After about 400 yards cross a stile. This footpath is S23 (Dodpits Lane). It goes through a copse into a field. Keep to the left of this. After about 400 yards turn left onto a track. When two houses come into view, turn right over grass with a large pond on your right. Follow the track round the pond and cross the stile at the end. Continue up to the road (Dodpits Lane). Cross the road by

Churchill Cottages and go up a track some 300 yards, then turn left. After about 600 yards, cross the stile and walk slightly to your right. Head towards the copse before you and after 400 yards, with the copse on your right, cross the stile, then turn slightly to your left and climb the field to the top left-hand corner. There, follow the fence turning right. With the fence on your left, in about 80 yards turn left for 500 yards or so. When you come to a sign-post, turn right and follow the path downwards towards some houses. There, just on a right-hand bend, go straight ahead over a footbridge and on to a road. Turn left there and continue for 700 yards when you will find the Church on the right.

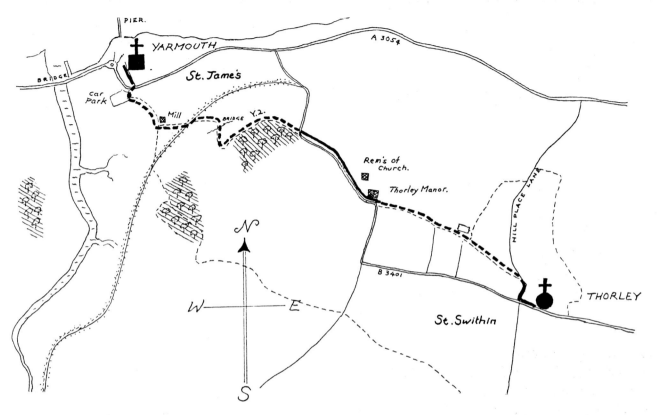

32. ST SWITHIN'S, Thorley, to ST JAMES, Yarmouth   1.5 miles

When you come out of the churchyard, turn right and after about 100 yards right again into Hill Place Lane. Follow the road about 150 yards to the Public Footpath, cross the field and over several stiles with Thorley Manor on the right and through main house gate (painted white), a distance in total of about half a mile. Turn right on road and continue for 50 yards with the ruins of St Swithin's Church on your right. Continue on road for a further 200 yards, take Public Footpath Y2 on your left through gate. Carry on through further gate and bear right across a stile. Continue on and over two more stiles with a bridge in between, and a further stile until you reach the old Railway Track. Turn left and in 20 yards turn right past the Old Mill house. Turn right again, follow path along bank of River Yar to Car Park entrance by school. Turn right, cross over main road and take next turning on your left - St James Street. The Church is about 100 yards on your right.

St Swithin, Thorley

This church was built by subscription in 1871; and was consecrated by Dr Wilberforce, Bishop of Winchester, on December 9th of that year. Its two bells are thought to have come from Shalfleet. The font (probably 13th century) came from the old church it replaced; similarly the altar table (17th century) now in the vestry. The Church Register going back to 1614 is also in the modern church.

The walls of the churchyard are built from the stones of the former structure. This had fallen into disrepair because most of the parishioners had moved to the east. Thus it was dismantled last century but the porch and belfry were deliberately preserved as a memorial; the old churchyard, too, in which they stand.

Little is known of the old church other than that it was founded by Amicia, Countess of Devon in the 13th century. It appears to have been a small church serving a sparsely populated rural area, the main activity of which was the raising of rabbits, and providing at one time some 500 a year, a valuable source of meat and fur.

Old Barn, Wellow

Old church remains

St James, Yarmouth

V. Vivian

This church was built between 1614 and 1626, and was consecrated by the Bishop of Salisbury. There exists an ancient record indicating that at one time there were two churches in this area even before 1200, but these have long since been demolished. The present tower was increased by 30 feet in 1831 as a memorial to a son of the architect, and also as a sea-mark.

Inside the church is the usual chancel and two-aisled nave. On the north side is a Lady Chapel, and on the south a mortuary chapel for the Holmes family. This contains a white marble statue of Sir Robert Holmes, Governor of the Island from 1668 to 1692. If the style of this statue strikes you as rather ornate, it is because it was originally intended for the glory of none other than the French King Louis XIV. However, the statue, finished apart from the head, was on its way to France when sculpture and sculptor fell into the hands of the English. Sir Robert thereupon coerced the sculptor to finish his work, but the Governor of the Isle of Wight became the model rather than the illustrious Sun King!

The only memorial in the Lady Chapel is to Elizabeth Morgan, daughter of Lieutenant Governor Anthony Morgan. It seems there was much ill feeling between this family and that of Sir Robert's, yet representatives from each now lie separated only by yards, and within the same hallowed place.

There are many stained glass windows here, and most have been given comparatively recently in memory of relatives. There is a matching pair of two-light windows in the Sanctuary, in memory of Henry Leigh and his wife, and their three children. They depict scenes from the Bible which in no way relate to their subjects.

The most colourful window is one of six lights over the altar. The inner four depict scenes from the Gospels, and the outer ones carry quotations from the Beatitudes - Blessed are the poor in heart, and Blessed are the meek for they shall see God. Special mention must be made of a very delicate and beautiful ceramic plaque in the style of Della Robia, the celebrated Dutch ceramicist.

River Yar at Yarmouth

From the Church, walk along Bridge Road, continue to the Roundabout and over Bridge. Take first turning on left (PF F1), turn right after about 400 yards, pass through a copse, cross a stile and along the edge of a field. At the end of this field, cross a stile, keeping the copse to your right. Continue downhill for 100 yards. Turn right, over a stile and footbridge and in 30 yards you come to a wide farm track. Take PF F8 Norton Green. Continue up the middle of the field, over a stile with wide gateway to a long narrow field which meets the road at Norton Green. Take the road opposite, passing the picturesque cottages of Norton Green, then take PF F14 on the left. Continue uphill through two wooden gates.

Keep to your left past the Holiday Camp. When at the top there are three grass paths. Keep to the centre, widest path. Carry on downhill for 150 yards when the pathway merges with a shingle track which bends round to the right. Follow track slightly uphill, with seats on your right for resting and viewing, and continue to its end.

Turn left, walk downhill for about 700 yards to the bottom. Turn right and then left again (Bridle Road to School Green). Walk to main road, cross over and in 30 yards take footpath F21. Go

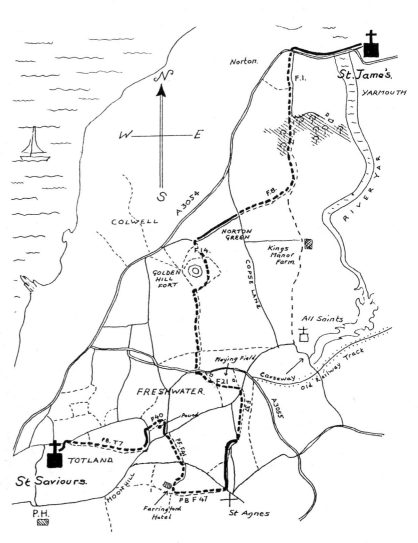

alongside red brick wall and across Playing Field to far corner. Cross the road (F37) through black metal gate with cottages one side and a stone building on the other. Continue along footpath over several stiles to Easton Lane. Turn right and go uphill, turn left at the top into Victoria Road and continue to end. Turn left and then immediately right (BP F47). Carry on uphill for 400 yards to green gate on right and trellised bridge straight ahead. Go through green gate into Farringford Hotel grounds and stay for tea! (Once the home of Alfred Lord Tennyson.) Continue down drive and at Hotel's main gate turn left for a few yards, cross road and take PF F41. Take this path to Pound Green with its historic pound. Continue round into F40 through left hand side of the field and in 250 yards turn left into Summers Lane. At the end of the lane turn right into Bedbury Lane and continue along the road for 50 yards. At BP T7 turn right and go up and downhill for 400 yards, over a stile and join Public Footpath. Carry on through a copse and through middle of a field to Summers Lane. Turn left and after 100 yards you arrive at St Saviour's Church.

The Farringford, formerly Tennyson's home

St Saviour's Roman Catholic Church, Totland Bay

This attractively designed church was erected in 1923, mainly through a legacy of Granville Ward from the nearby Weston Manor.*

The architect, James Mangan, is thought to have based his design on a small church in Rome. The brickwork, especially the interior, is considered by many to be one of the finest examples on the Island of the bricklayer's art. The builders were Messrs. Privett.

* Weston Manor, with its own private Chapel, was built in 1871 by William George Ward (the family also owning Northwood House, Cowes). It is now run by a Religious Order as a home for men with learning difficulties.

The Island's only thatched church

Pilgrim's Diary

Walk No.	From	To	Date undertaken	Notes

Pilgrim's Diary

Walk No.	From	To	Date undertaken	Notes

Pilgrim's Diary

Walk No.	From	To	Date undertaken	Notes

Pilgrim's Diary

Walk No.	From	To	Date undertaken	Notes

Pilgrim's Diary

Walk No.	From	To	Date undertaken	Notes